Super-cute Doorstops

35 charming doorstops that bring character to any room

Emma Hardy

CICO BOOKS

LONDON NEW YORK

www.cicobooks.com

Published in 2012 by CICO Books
An imprint of Ryland Peters & Small Ltd

20–21 Jockey's Fields   519 Broadway, 5th Floor
London WC1R 4BW   New York, NY 10012

www.cicobooks.com

10 9 8 7 6 5 4 3 2 1

A CIP catalog record for this book is available from the
Library of Congress and the British Library.

ISBN: 978 1 908170 93 4

Printed in China

Editor: Sarah Hoggett
Designer: Louise Leffler
Photographer: Debbie Patterson
Illustrator: Michael Hill
Stylist: Emma Hardy

RPS CICO BOOKS
For digital editions, visit
www.cicobooks.com/apps.php

Super-cute
Doorstops

Contents

Introduction

Step into any gift and home furnishing store and you are likely to find an array of different doorstops for sale. While there are lots of lovely designs available, it is much more fun and economical to make them yourself—and surprisingly easy. In this book, there are 35 different doorstops and draft excluders to make, with prettily illustrated step-by-step instructions to help you along the way.

Each project gives quantities for fabric and a list of any other materials that you will need. As well as these specific materials, it is a good idea to put together a basic sewing kit that will be useful for all of the projects. A good pair of dressmaking scissors is a must; a pair of scissors for cutting paper, a selection of needles in different sizes, a tape measure, pins, and spools of cotton thread in a few colors will all be useful.

Before you start, turn to the techniques section for tips on making and filling your doorstops, to help you decide on the most suitable filling as well as for help with specific stitches and technical terms. Lots of fabrics can be used for making doorstops and draft excluders, although very lightweight ones should be avoided. None of the projects require large pieces of fabric and most of them can be made using scraps and remnants of cloth.

Whether you are making a doorstop for yourself or as a gift, there are plenty of ideas here, with designs for all ages and tastes. From doorstops for children such as the bunny fairy and rocket to more sophisticated ones such as the pyramids and velvet ball, I hope you will find lots of projects to inspire you.

Chapter One
Cute Creatures

Chunky chicken

Choose fabric with a retro feel for this chunky chicken doorstop. Make the beak and comb in a bright, contrasting color of felt so that they really stand out, and stitch big buttons onto either side of the head for eyes.

You will need

Patterns on page 112

40 x 32 in. (100 x 80 cm) medium-weight iron-on interfacing

40 x 32 in. (100 x 80 cm) fabric

6 x 6 in. (15 x 15 cm) coordinating felt

Polyester toy filling or kapok

Dried peas or similar

Two buttons, approx. ¾ in. (2 cm) in diameter, for eyes

Take ⅜-in. (1-cm) seam allowances throughout, unless otherwise stated.

1. Following the manufacturer's instructions, apply interfacing to the wrong side of the fabric. Enlarge the patterns on page 112 to twice the size and cut out. Cut two bodies and one base piece from fabric, and one beak and one comb from felt.

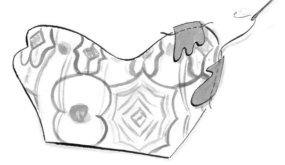

2. Pin the beak and comb to the right side of one of the body pieces, facing inward. Baste (tack) them in place.

3. With right sides together, pin and machine stitch the body shapes together, leaving the straight bottom edge open. Snip the seam allowance (see page 109), turn right side out, and press.

4. Turn the body wrong side out again and pin the base in place, with right sides together. Machine stitch, leaving a gap of about 2½ in. (6 cm). Make small snips around the seam allowance and turn right side out. Press.

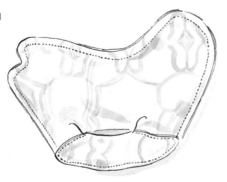

5. Fill the chicken about two thirds full with polyester toy filling or kapok, taking care to push it into the tail and head. Fill the remaining space with dried peas or similar (see page 110). Whipstitch the gap closed (see page 111). Sew a button eye to either side of the chicken's head to finish.

Bunny fairy

A lovely doorstop for a child's bedroom, this charming bunny fairy is cute and practical at the same time. Choose a brightly colored gingham fabric for the skirt and make a big bow shape for the wings to stitch onto the back. Because the bunny is tall and thin, be sure to fill her with enough dried peas to stand up well.

You will need

Patterns on page 112

28 x 24 in. (70 x 60 cm) medium-weight iron-on interfacing

24 x 6 in. (60 x 15 cm) cream fabric

22 x 12 in. (55 x 30 cm) striped fabric

9 in. (22 cm) coordinating rickrack braid

Embroidery floss (thread) in blue and pink

Polyester toy filling or kapok

Dried peas or similar

46 x 8 in. (115 x 20 cm) gingham fabric

Button ⅝ in. (1.5 cm) in diameter for dress

1½-in. (4-cm) square piece of felt

Button ⅜ in. (1 cm) in diameter for ear

Take ⅜-in. (1-cm) seam allowances throughout, unless otherwise stated.

1. Following the manufacturer's instructions, apply interfacing to the wrong side of the cream and striped fabrics. Enlarge the pattern pieces on page 112 to twice the size and cut out. Cut two head pieces and four ear pieces from cream fabric and two body pieces and one base piece from striped fabric.

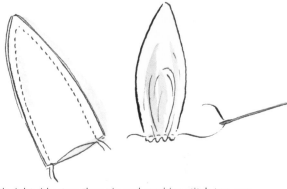

2. With right sides together, pin and machine stitch two ear pieces together, leaving the straight bottom edge open. Trim the seam allowance to ¼ in. (5 mm) and turn right side out. Press. Work a line of running stitch (see page 111) along the bottom edge and pull the thread to gather the ear slightly. Secure with a few small stitches. Repeat with the two remaining ear pieces.

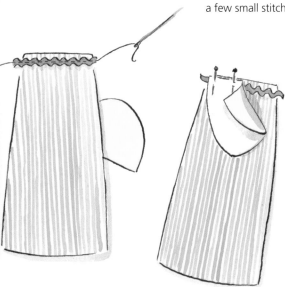

3. Cut the rickrack braid in half. Pin and baste (tack) one length along the top edge of each body piece on the right side, about ¼ in. (5 mm) from the edge. With right sides together, pin and machine stitch a head piece to each body piece, stitching along the center of the rickrack. Press the seam toward the body, then press the front so that the rickrack sits along the top of the body (the striped fabric).

4. Using blue embroidery floss (thread), work two French knots (see page 111) for eyes. Using pink floss (thread), work three straight stitches of different lengths for the nose and three whiskers at either side.

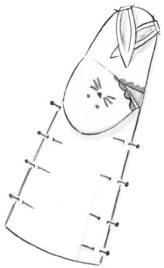

5. Pin and baste (tack) the ears to the top of the head on one of the bunny pieces, leaving a gap of about ⅝ in. (1.5 cm) between the two ears. With right sides together, pin and machine stitch the two bunny pieces together, leaving the straight bottom edge open. Make a few small snips in the seam allowance around the head (see page 109) and turn right side out. Press.

6. Turn the bunny wrong side out again. With right sides together, pin and machine stitch the base around the bottom edge, leaving a gap of about 2½ in. (6 cm) along the back edge. Turn right side out again and press around the bottom. Fill the bunny about half full with polyester toy filling or kapok, then fill the remaining space with dried peas or similar (see page 110). Whipstitch the gap closed (see page 111).

7. Cut a 23½ x 6⅜-in. (60 x 16-cm) rectangle of gingham fabric for the skirt. With right sides together, pin and machine stitch the two short ends together to form a loop. Press the seam open. Turn the bottom edge to the wrong side by ⅜ in. (1 cm) and press, and then by another ⅜ in. (1 cm). Machine stitch.

8. Work a line of running stitch along the top edge and pull the thread to gather it slightly. Put the skirt on the bunny, pulling the thread so that it fits snugly around the body, and hand stitch it in place, using a neat running stitch.

9. Cut a piece of gingham fabric measuring 10¼ x 2⅜ in. (26 x 6 cm). Fold it in half, right sides together, aligning the two long sides. Machine stitch along one short end and along the raw long edge. Snip off the corner seam allowance, turn right side out, and press. Put this band around the top of the skirt on the bunny and stitch the ends together, tucking the raw short end neatly under the stitched end. Whipstitch along the band to attach it to the bunny and hold it in place.

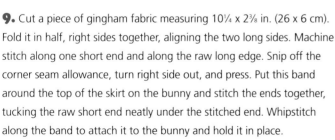

10. Cut a 7½-in. (19-cm) square piece of gingham. Fold it in half, right sides together, and machine stitch along the raw edges, leaving a gap of about 1½ in. (4 cm) in the middle of the long side. Snip off the corner seam allowances, turn right side out, and press. Whipstitch the gap closed.

11. Cut another piece of gingham measuring 2¾ x 2⅜ in. (7 x 6 cm). Fold it in half, wrong sides together, aligning the long sides. Machine stitch along the long edge, turn right side out, and press. Wrap this piece around the middle of the first piece to look like a bow and whipstitch the ends together neatly. Sew the bow onto the back of the bunny, with the neat side of the bow facing outward.

12. Stitch a button onto the waistband of the skirt for decoration. Using the pattern on page 115, cut a small flower from felt. Hand stitch it onto one of the ears with a button at its center.

Cat

This cuddly cat is easy to make and adds a charming, cozy touch to any room. Tweed fabric gives it a lovely woolly look, but any fabrics could be used. For the patches, either choose a fabric for the patches that will not fray or, if the fabric has a loose weave, use fusible bonding web to fix them in place.

You will need

Patterns on page 113

32 x 20 in. (80 x 50 cm) medium-weight iron-on interfacing

32 x 20 in. (80 x 50 cm) solid-color wool fabric

Polyester toy filling or kapok

Dried peas or similar

12 x 8 in. (30 x 20 cm) plaid wool fabric

Brown embroidery floss (thread)

12½ in. (31 cm) ribbon, ⅜ in. (1 cm) wide

Three buttons for eyes and nose, approx. ⅝ in. (1.5 cm) in diameter

Button for name tag, approx. ¾ in. (2 cm) in diameter

Take ⅜-in. (1-cm) seam allowances throughout, unless otherwise stated.

1. Following the manufacturer's instructions, apply interfacing to the wrong side of the solid-color wool fabric. Enlarge the patterns on page 113 to twice the size and cut out. Cut two bodies, one base, and two tails from the solid-color wool fabric.

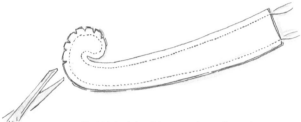

2. With right sides together, pin and machine stitch the tail pieces together, leaving the straight end open. Make small snips around the seam allowance (see page 109) and turn right side out. Press and fill with polyester toy filling or kapok, leaving about ¾ in. (2 cm) unfilled at the open end.

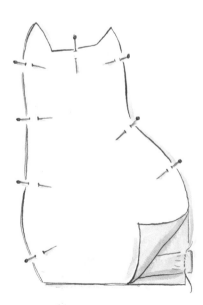

3. Aligning the raw edges, pin and baste (tack) the tail onto the right side of one of the body pieces. With right sides together, pin and machine stitch the second body piece to the first, leaving the bottom edge open. Make small snips in the seam allowance around the curves and turn right side out. Press.

4. Turn wrong side out again. Pin and machine stitch the base in place, leaving a 4-in. (10-cm) gap along the back, and turn right side out. Fill the cat about two thirds full with polyester toy filling or kapok, then fill the remaining space with dried peas or similar (see page 110). Pack the peas in tightly, then whipstitch the gap closed (see page 111).

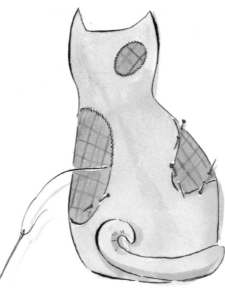

5. Enlarge the patch patterns on page 113 to twice the size and cut out. Cut the three patches from plaid wool fabric. Pin them onto the cat and overstitch them in place. Sew the tail onto the front of the cat, securing it with a few stitches toward the tip.

6. Take a length of brown embroidery floss (thread) and tie a knot about 2½ in. (6 cm) from the end. Stitch through the cat's face and tie another knot where the floss comes out of the face. Trim both ends to 2 in. (5 cm) to make the first whisker. Repeat twice more to make three whiskers on each side of the face. Wrap the ribbon around the neck to form the collar and stitch the ends together at the back. Sew buttons in place for the eyes, nose, and name tag.

Dylan dog

It's hard not to fall for this adorable dog doorstop, who comes complete with hat and sweater. He may not be the best guard dog, but he's certain to get lots of attention if you position him near your front door. I opted for button eyes, but you could use decorative embroidery stitches or felt appliqué.

You will need

Patterns on page 114

40 x 20 in. (100 x 50 cm) medium-weight iron-on interfacing

32 x 20 in. (80 x 50 cm) brown wool fabric

8 x 12 in. (20 x 30 cm) tweed fabric for ears

Polyester toy filling or kapok

Dried peas or similar

Two buttons, ⅝ in. (1.5 cm) in diameter, for eyes

Button, 1¼ in. (3 cm) in diameter, for nose

Pair of socks for the sweater

One sock for the hat

Yarn

Cardstock

Take ⅜-in. (1-cm) seam allowances throughout, unless otherwise stated.

1. Following the manufacturer's instructions, apply interfacing to the wrong side of the wool fabric. Enlarge the patterns on page 114 to twice this size. Cut two bodies, one head, one base, two end pieces, two tails, and four eight legs from the wool fabric. Cut four ear pieces from tweed fabric (they do not need interfacing).

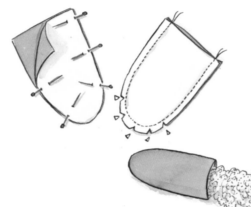

2. With right sides together, pin and machine stitch two leg pieces together, cut small snips in the seam allowance (see page 109), and turn right side out. Repeat with the other leg pieces to make four legs. Do the same with the two tail pieces. Push a little toy filling or kapok into each leg.

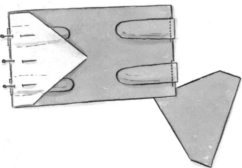

3. Aligning the raw edges, pin and baste (tack) two legs to the right side of each short end of the base piece, positioning the legs ¾ in. (2 cm) in from the long edges. With right sides together, pin and machine stitch an end piece to each end of the base. Press the seams open.

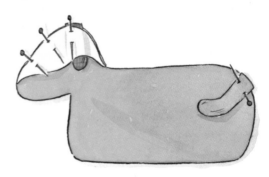

4. Pin and baste (tack) the tail onto one of the body pieces where marked on the pattern. With right sides together, pin and machine stitch two ear pieces together, make small snips in the seam allowance, and turn right side out. Repeat to make the second ear. Pin and baste (tack) one ear to each body piece. With right sides together, pin and stitch the head to one of the body pieces.

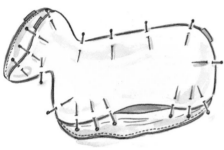

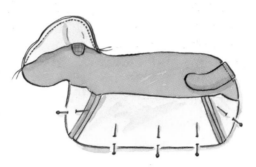

5. With right sides together, pin and machine stitch the base onto the body piece with the head. Press the seam open.

6. With right sides together, pin and machine stitch the second body piece to this, leaving a gap of about 3 in. (8 cm) along the bottom edge. Make small snips around the curves and press the seams open. Turn right side out.

7. Fill the dog about two thirds full with polyester toy filling or kapok, pushing it into the face and corners, then fill the remaining space with dried peas or similar (see page 110). Whipstitch the gap closed (see page 111). Sew buttons in place for the eyes and nose.

8. To make the sweater, cut off a section about 6 in. (15 cm) long from each sock and cut them open to make two flat pieces. With right sides together, pin and machine stitch the two pieces together along the long edges, leaving a 2-in. (5-cm) gap in the middle of one seam. Turn the raw edge over to the wrong side by ⅜ in. (1 cm) and machine stitch to hem. Push the sweater onto the dog, putting the front legs through the opening in the seam.

9. To make the hat, cut 4½ in. (11 cm) off the top of the third sock. Turn this section inside out and work a line of running stitch around the raw edge. Pull the thread to gather, and secure with a few small stitches. Make a pom-pom following the instructions on page 105 and sew it to the top of the hat, over the gathering stitches. Pull the hat onto the dog's head, pulling it over the ears slightly, and secure with a few small stitches.

Appliquéd robot

You will need

Patterns on page 115

8 x 4 in. (20 x 10 cm) striped fabric

8 x 4 in. (20 x 10 cm) gingham fabric

24-in. (60-cm) square of fusible bonding web

24 x 12 in. (60 x 30 cm) red fabric

Scraps of red and blue fabrics

32 x 20 in. (80 x 50 cm) medium-weight iron-on interfacing

32 x 20 in. (80 x 50 cm) blue fabric

One button, ⅝ in. (17 mm) in diameter, for control panel

Two white buttons, ⅜ in. (1 cm) in diameter, for control panel

Polyester toy filling or kapok

Dried peas or similar

Two buttons, ⅝ in. (1.5 cm) in diameter, for eyes

Two colored buttons, ⅜ in. (1 cm) in diameter, for ears

Take ⅜-in. (1-cm) seam allowances throughout, unless otherwise stated.

Appliqué is a great way to create decoration on a plain block doorstop, and this robot design is really fun to do. Attach the shapes to the backing fabric with fusible bonding web, machine or hand stitching around all the edges as well if you like.

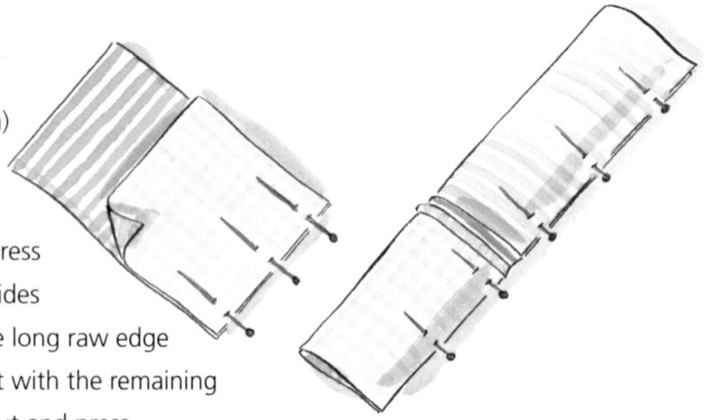

1. Cut two 3½ x 2⅛-in. (9 x 5.5-cm) pieces of striped fabric and two 3 x 2⅛-in. (7.5 x 5.5-cm) pieces of gingham fabric. With right sides together, pin and machine stitch a gingham piece to a striped piece along one short side. Press the seam open. Fold in half lengthwise, right sides together, and pin and machine stitch along the long raw edge and one short end. Cut off the corners. Repeat with the remaining two pieces to make two legs. Turn right side out and press.

2. Following the manufacturer's instructions, apply fusible bonding web to the wrong side of the red, striped, and gingham fabrics and the scraps of red and blue fabrics. From red fabric, cut three 3⅛ x 2⅜-in. (8 x 6-cm) rectangles for the head panels, two 2⅜-in. (6-cm) squares for the side head panels, one 5½ x 4¾-in. (14 x 12-cm) rectangle for the front panel, and two 5½ x 4-in. (14 x 10-cm) rectangles for the side body panels.

3. Enlarge the patterns on page 115 to twice the size and cut out. Cut two arms, two hands, two large ear circles, two small ear circles, one mouth, and the control panels from scraps of different fabrics.

4. Following the manufacturer's instructions, apply interfacing to the wrong side of the blue fabric. For the robot's body, cut two 8¼ x 6⅝-in. (21 x 17-cm) rectangles for the front and back, two 8¼ x 5½-in. (21 x 14-cm) rectangles for the sides, and two 8¼ x 5½-in. (21 x 14-cm) rectangles for the top and bottom.

5. With right sides together, pin and machine stitch one blue side body piece to each long edge of the blue front body piece. Press the seams open. Pin and machine stitch the blue back body piece onto one side to form a strip. Press the seam open.

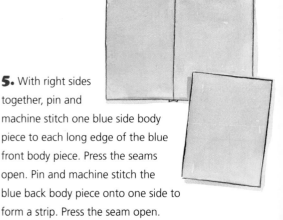

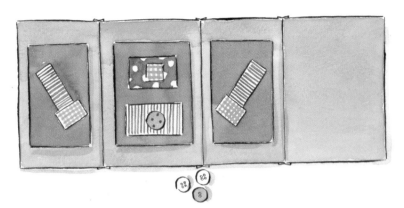

6. Peel the backing papers from the fabrics from steps 2 and 3. Center the red front and side panels on the blue front and side pieces, place a damp cloth on top, and press with a warm iron. Position the arms, hands, and control panels in the correct places and apply them in the same way. Stitch the buttons in place on the control panels.

7. With right sides together, pin the blue top body piece in place, matching the corners with the seams of the body. Machine stitch, starting and finishing sewing ⅜ in. (1 cm) from the outer edges, and cut a snip at each corner. Turn right side out and press.

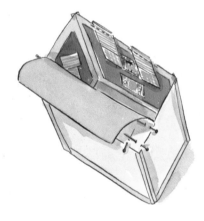

8. Pin and baste (tack) the legs to the front of the body at the bottom, placing them 1¼ in. (3 cm) from the outer edge. Turn the body wrong side out again and pin and machine stitch the blue base onto the body in the same way as the top, leaving a gap of about 3 in. (8 cm) along the back. Turn right side out and press.

9. Fill the body about two thirds full with polyester toy filling or kapok, then fill the remaining space with dried peas or similar (see page 110). Whipstitch the gap closed (see page 111).

10. To make the head, cut four 4¾ x 4-in. (12 x 10-cm) rectangles and two 4-in. (10-cm) squares for the sides of the head from blue fabric. With right sides together, pin and machine stitch the rectangles together along the long sides to form a long strip. Press the seams open.

11. Center the three red head panels on three of the blue rectangles and press in place. Center the two red head side panels centrally on the blue head side pieces and press in place. Arrange the fabric ears and mouth on the head and press in place as before. Sew buttons in place for the eyes and ears.

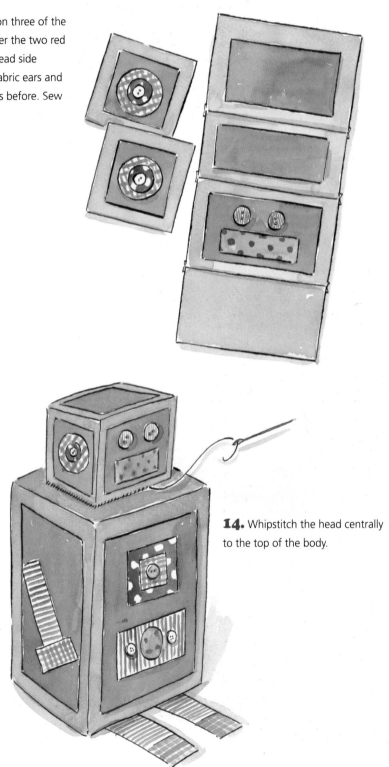

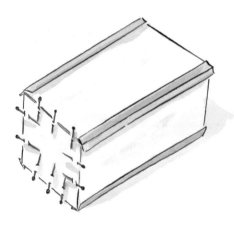

12. With right sides together, pin and machine stitch the two short sides of the long head strip together to make a tube. Press the seam open. With right sides together, pin and machine stitch one of the side pieces to one of the ends in the same way as before. Turn right side out and press.

13. Turn the robot wrong side out again. With right sides together, pin and machine stitch the second head side piece in place, leaving a gap of about 2 in. (5 cm) along the bottom edge. Snip the corners, turn right side out, and press. Fill the head with polyester toy filling or kapok and whipstitch the gap closed.

14. Whipstitch the head centrally to the top of the body.

Russian doll

This lovely lady is such a cutie, she is sure to be adored by all who see her. Use whatever ribbon or braid you have to embellish her, embroidering a simple face or using small buttons for the eyes and cheeks as an alternative.

1. Following the manufacturer's instructions, apply interfacing to the wrong side of both pieces of fabric. Enlarge the patterns on page 115 to twice the size. Cut two heads, two bodies, and one base piece from the appropriate fabrics.

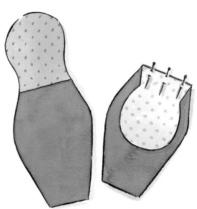

2. With right sides together, pin and machine stitch a head to a body section and press the seam open. Repeat with the remaining two pieces.

3. Using the pattern on page 115, cut out the apron, six large flowers, two leaves, and two small flowers from scraps of felt. Stitch four of the large flowers onto the apron by sewing a French knot (see page 111) at the center of each one using embroidery floss (thread). Sew the leaves in place with a few small stitches.

4. Pin and baste (tack) the rickrack braid onto the wrong side of the apron around the curved edge, to form a scalloped edging. Pin and machine stitch around the curve of the apron onto one of the doll pieces; this will become the front of the doll. Pin the length of ribbon across the top of the apron to form the strap, stitching along the top and bottom edges of the ribbon.

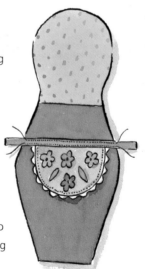

Patterns on page 115

20 x 26 in. (50 x 65 cm) medium-weight iron-on interfacing

12 x 26 in. (30 x 65 cm) fabric for the body and base

8 x 16 in. (20 x 40 cm) fabric for the head

Scraps of felt for the apron, flowers, leaves, and hair

Embroidery floss (thread) for the eyes, mouth, cheeks, and flowers

10 in. (25 cm) each of two colors of rickrack braid, ribbon, pom-pom trim, and braid for the apron

4-in. (10-cm) square of flesh-colored felt

Polyester toy filling or kapok

Dried peas or similar

Take ⅜-in. (1-cm) seam allowances throughout, unless otherwise stated.

5. Cut a circle 3 in. (7 cm) in diameter from flesh-colored felt. Using the pattern on page 115, cut two pieces of felt for the hair. Pin the hair in place and overstitch around the inside edge to hold it in place. Using embroidery floss (thread), stitch two eyes and two cheeks in satin stitch and a small mouth in backstitch (see page 111).

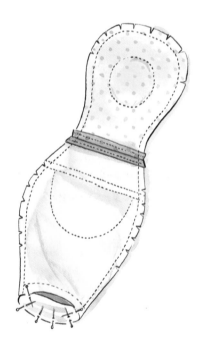

6. Pin the face to the front of the doll and overstitch around the edge with small, neat stitches. Pin and machine stitch rickrack braid over the seam between the top and bottom sections, a length of braid just under the rickrack, and a length of pom-pom trim about 1½ in. (4 cm) up from the bottom edge. Sew the remaining felt flowers onto the head with a French knot using embroidery floss (thread), placing the small flowers in the center of the large ones.

7. With right sides together, pin and machine stitch the front of the doll to the back, leaving the bottom edge open. Make small snips in the seam allowance around the curves (see page 109) and turn right side out. Press.

8. Turn the doll wrong side out again. With right sides together, pin and machine stitch the base to the bottom of the doll, leaving a gap of about 5 in. (12 cm) at the back. Turn right side out again and press around the bottom.

9. Fill the doll about two thirds full with polyester toy filling or kapok, then fill the remaining space with dried peas or similar (see page 110). Whipstitch the gap closed (see page 111).

Dotty dachshund

This classic dachshund, made from delightfully dotty fabric, is simple to make and great fun, too. Button eyes and a pom-pom nose give it a really cute expression.

You will need

Patterns on page 116

53 x 33½ in. (135 x 85 cm) medium-weight iron-on interfacing

53 x 33½ in. (135 x 85 cm) main fabric

24 x 8 in. (60 x 20 cm) coordinating fabric

Polyester toy filling or kapok

Dried peas or similar

14½ x ¾ in. (37 x 2 cm) felt for collar

Button, ¾ in. (2 cm) in diameter for name tag

4 x 3¼ in. (10 x 8 cm) white felt

Two buttons, approx. ⅝ in. (1.5 cm) in diameter, for eyes

Small pom-pom

Take ⅜-in. (1-cm) seam allowances throughout, unless otherwise stated.

1. Following the manufacturer's instructions, apply interfacing to the wrong side of the main fabric. Enlarge the patterns on page 116 to twice the size and cut out. Cut two dog shapes (using the head, tail, and a rectangle in between) and one base piece.

2. Cut four ears from the coordinating fabric. With right sides together, pin and machine stitch two ears together, leaving the straight side open. Cut small snips in the seam allowance (see page 109) and turn right side out. Press, turning the raw edge inside the ear by ⅜ in. (1 cm). Repeat with the remaining two ear pieces.

3. Pin and machine stitch one ear to the right side of each dog piece, as indicated on the pattern. Pin and stitch them upside down, so that the stitch line cannot be seen.

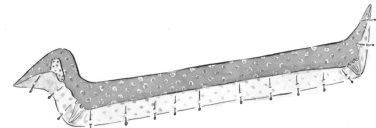

4. With right sides together, pin and machine stitch the base to one of the dog pieces, aligning the end of the base with the tip of the nose. Make a small snip at the corners and a few small snips in the seam allowance around the curves.

5. With right sides together, pin and machine stitch the second dog shape to the base in the same way, leaving a gap of about 6 in. (15 cm) in the center of the bottom edge. Snip the seam allowance and turn right side out. Press.

6. Fill the dog about three quarters full with polyester toy filling or kapok, making sure that the head and tail are well stuffed, then fill the remaining space with dried peas or similar, ensuring that they fill the length of the body (see page 110). Whipstitch the gap closed (see page 111).

7. Stitch the felt strip around the neck to make a collar and sew a button under the chin for a name tag. Using the pattern on page 116, cut two eyes from white felt and stitch a button to the center of each one. Stitch the eyes onto the head using small straight stitches. Hand stitch the pom-pom onto the tip of the nose, stitching through it several times to hold it securely in place.

Sock monster

Choose a brightly colored sock for this funny monster doorstop, which can be personalized with a bold initial cut from felt. Hand-draw a letter on paper and use it as your pattern or print the initial from your computer, enlarging it on a photocopier if necessary. Get the recipient involved in making funny googly eyes and a crazy haircut.

1. Push polyester toy filling or kapok into the sock until it is about two thirds full, then pour in dried peas, leaving about 2 in. (5 cm) unfilled at the top (see page 110). If you are using a very long sock, you may want to cut off the top to prevent your monster from becoming too tall and skinny.

2. Work a line of running stitch (see page 111) around the top end of the sock about ⅝ in. (1.5 cm) from the top and pull the thread to gather it, pushing the end inside to make a neat bottom. Loosen the stitches and pour in more dried peas if necessary and then gather tightly again and sew a few secure stitches to hold everything in place.

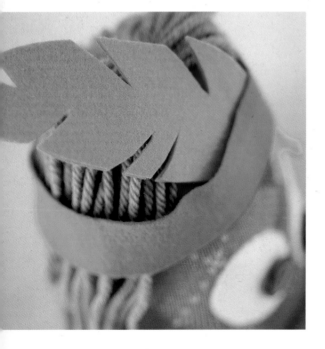

3. Pull the heel of the sock out a little and fold the middle of it in to form a mouth. Stitch through the lips, starting and finishing with a few small stitches to hold it in place.

4. Cut out a felt letter for the initial. Pin it onto the monster and sew it in place, using small, straight stitches around the edge. Enlarge the pattern on page 116 to twice the size and cut two eyes from white felt. Sew a button onto each one, placing them at angles to give the monster a googly-eyed look, then pin and stitch the eyes in place.

5. Thread a tapestry needle with yarn and stitch through the top of the head. Cut the yarn on either side to make the first strand of hair; repeat until the monster has a full head of hair.

6. Enlarge the pattern on page 116 to twice the size and cut out a paper feather shape. Glue two pieces of orange felt together and, when dry, pin the feather pattern onto the felt and cut out. Stitch the feather onto the forehead at an angle with a few small stitches. Wrap the strip of blue felt around the head, overlap the ends, and stitch them together. Sew a few small stitches at the front to hold the headband in place.

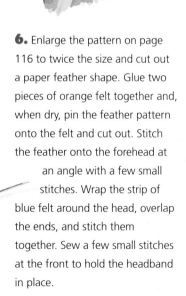

Mrs Mouse

To make this marvelous mouse doorstop, I chose a solid-colored fabric for the body with a delicate floral print for the apron, but a patterned fabric for the body would look very pretty, too. To make a mouse for a boy, simply omit the apron and the bow on the head and stitch a ribbon bow onto the front for a bow tie.

You will need

Patterns on page 117

36 x 16 in. (90 x 40 cm) gray fabric

36 x 16 in. (90 x 40 cm) medium-weight iron-on interfacing

12 x 1¼ in. (30 x 3 cm) pink fabric

Pipe cleaner

26 x 8 in. (65 x 20 cm) floral fabric for apron

Polyester toy filling or kapok

Dried peas or similar

Fusible bonding web

Pink embroidery floss (thread)

8 in. (20 cm) ribbon, ⅝ in. (1.5 cm) wide

Take ⅜-in. (1-cm) seam allowances throughout, unless otherwise stated.

1. Enlarge the patterns on page 117 to twice the size and cut out. Cut four outer ears from the gray fabric. Following the manufacturer's instructions, apply interfacing to the wrong side of the remaining gray fabric.

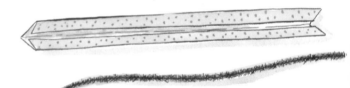

2. Cut a 9 x 1½-in. (23 x 4-cm) strip of pink fabric for the tail. Fold it in half lengthwise and press. Open the fabric out again and fold one short end to the wrong side by ⅜ in. (1 cm). Fold each long side in to the center crease, fold along the center crease, and press again. Machine stitch along the length and across the folded short end. Bend the end of the pipe cleaner over to blunt the end. Cut the pipe cleaner to 8¾ in. (22 cm) and push it inside the tail.

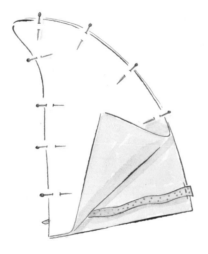

3. Cut two body shapes and one base from gray fabric. Pin and baste (tack) the tail to the right side of one of the body pieces, ¾ in. (2 cm) from the bottom. Curl the tail around to keep it out of the way while you are sewing. With right sides together, pin and machine stitch the body pieces together, leaving the straight edge open. Trim the seam allowance around the nose and cut small snips in the seam allowance around the curved areas (see page 109). Turn right side out and press.

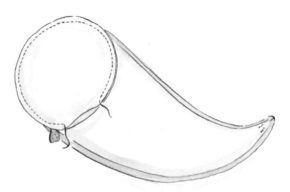

4. Thread an embroidery needle with pink floss (thread) and tie a knot in the end. Work two French knots (see page 111) for the eyes. Tie another knot in the end of the floss, bring the needle through the mouse's cheek from the wrong side, and cut the floss to about ¾ in. (2 cm) long to make a small whisker. Repeat so that there are three whiskers on each side of the face.

5. Turn the body wrong side out. With right sides together, pin and machine stitch the base in place, leaving a gap of about 3½ in. (9 cm) along the back. Make small snips in the seam allowance and turn right side out. Press.

6. Fill the mouse about two thirds full with polyester toy filling or kapok, making sure there are no lumps and bumps, then fill the remaining space with dried peas or similar (see page 110). Whipstitch the gap closed (see page 111).

7. Pin and machine stitch two gray outer ear pieces together, leaving the bottom edge open, them trim the seam allowance to about ¼ in. (5 mm) and turn right side out. Repeat with the other two gray ear pieces.

8. Following the manufacturer's instructions, apply fusible bonding web to the back of the pink fabric. Cut out two inner ears and press them onto the gray ears. Fold the bottom of the ears to the inside by ⅜ in. (1 cm) and press. Work a line of running stitch (see page 111) along the bottom of each ear and pull the thread to gather it slightly. Secure with a few small stitches, then sew the ears onto the mouse using small, neat stitches.

9. For the apron, cut an 8½ x 5½-in. (21 x 13-cm) rectangle of floral fabric. Fold over a double ⅜-in. (1-cm) hem to the wrong side along the two short sides and one long side, press, and machine stitch. Work a line of running stitch across the top raw edge and pull the thread to gather it to about 3 in. (7 cm). Finish with a few small stitches to hold it in place.

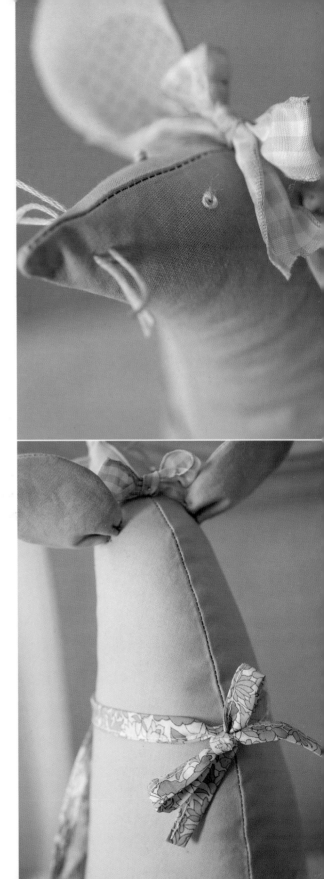

10. Cut a 24 x 1½-in. (60 x 4-cm) strip of floral fabric for the apron tie. Fold it in half lengthwise and press. Open it out again. Press both short ends under by ⅜ in. (1 cm), then fold both long edges in to the center crease line and press. Lay the apron centrally on the tie and baste (tack) it in place. Pin, topstitch along the tie close to the open edge, and press. Put the apron on the mouse, securing it in place with a few stitches if you like. Tie the ribbon in a neat bow and sew it onto the mouse's head, between the ears.

Owl

This wise old owl is made from bold, floral fabric giving it a bright, vintage feel. Colored felt cut into a scalloped shape forms the feathers, with two unmatching buttons making the eyes.

You will need

Patterns on page 117

32 x 16 in. (80 x 40 cm) floral fabric

32 x 16 in. (80 x 40 cm) medium-weight iron-on interfacing

Scraps of felt in bright colors

6 x 4 in. (15 x 10 cm) fusible bonding web

6 x 4 in. (15 x 10 cm) patterned fabric

Two buttons, approx. 1 in. (2.5 cm) in diameter

Polyester toy filling or kapok

Dried peas or similar

Take ⅜-in. (1-cm) seam allowances throughout, unless otherwise stated.

1. Enlarge the patterns on page 117 to twice the size and cut out. Following the manufacturer's instructions, apply interfacing to the wrong side of the floral fabric. Cut two bodies and one base from the floral fabric. Cut two flower-shaped eyes, two eye circles, one beak, two small feather shapes, and two long feather shapes from different colors of felt.

2. Following the manufacturer's instructions, apply fusible bonding web to the wrong side of the patterned fabric. Using the pattern on page 117, cut out an oval shape to go behind the eyes. Peel the backing paper from the bonding web and place the shape on the right side of one of the owl pieces. Lay a damp cloth over it and press with a warm iron.

3. Pin and machine stitch the feather shapes and the beak onto the owl. Hand stitch the eye circles onto the flower shapes, finishing with a button in the center of each eye, and hand stitch onto the owl, stitching through all the layers.

4. With right sides together, pin and machine stitch the two owl pieces together. Trim the seam allowance at the top of the ears. Turn right side out and press.

5. Turn the owl wrong side out again. Pin and machine stitch the base in place, leaving a 3-in. (8-cm) gap along the back. Turn right side out. Fill the owl about two thirds full with polyester toy filling or kapok, then fill the remaining space with dried peas or similar (see page 110). Whipstitch the gap closed (see page 111).

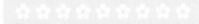

You will need

Patterns on page 118

44 x 27½ in. (110 x 70 cm) medium-weight iron-on interfacing

26 x 14 in. (65 x 35 cm) flesh-colored fabric

24 x 10 in. (60 x 25 cm) patterned fabric

16 x 7 in. (40 x 17 cm) striped fabric

6-in. (15-cm) square of solid-colored fabric

40 in. (100 cm) rickrack braid

Polyester toy filling or kapok

Dried peas or similar

Embroidery floss (thread) for eyes, nose, cheeks, and mouth

Yarn for hair

Ribbon for hair, ⅝ in. (1.5 cm) wide

Two buttons, approx. ¾ in. (2 cm) in diameter, for dress

Two buttons, approx. ⅝ in. (1.5 cm) in diameter, for shoes

Take ⅜-in. (1-cm) seam allowances throughout, unless otherwise stated.

Doll

This cute dolly doorstop looks so sweet sitting at the foot of a door. She can, of course, be made in any fabric—try a pretty floral print, with tiny ribbon bows instead of buttons on the shoes.

1. Following the manufacturer's instructions, apply interfacing to the wrong sides of all the fabrics. Enlarge the patterns on page 118 to twice the size and cut out. Cut two heads, four hands, and four legs from the flesh-colored fabric; two bodies and four arms from the patterned fabric; two skirts and one base from the striped fabric; and four shoes from the solid-colored fabric.

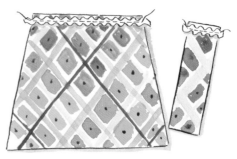

2. Cut two 7½-in. (19-cm) and two 2-in. (5-cm) lengths of rickrack braid. Pin and baste (tack) the long pieces to the body pieces and the short pieces to two of the arm pieces, ¼ in. (5 mm) from the top edge. Trim the edges of the rickrack braid level with the fabric.

3. With right sides together, pin and machine stitch the head pieces to the tops of the body pieces. Press the seams toward the heads. With right sides together, pin and machine stitch the hands to the arms. Press the seams toward the hands.

4. With right sides together, pin and machine stitch the skirts to the bottom edge of the bodies. Press the seams open. On the right side, baste (tack) and stitch 8¾ in. (22 cm) of rickrack braid along the seam on both pieces.

5. With right sides together, pin and machine stitch the shoes to the ends of the legs. Press the seams open. With right sides together, pin and machine stitch two of the legs together, leaving the top of the legs open. Make small snips in the seam allowance and turn right side out (see page 109). Press. Fill the legs with polyester toy filling or kapok, leaving about ¾ in. (2 cm) empty at the top. Repeat with the second two leg pieces and the four arm pieces.

6. Using a fadeaway fabric marker pen, draw the features on the doll's face. Split a length of embroidery floss (thread) into three strands. Thread an embroidery needle with the three strands and tie a knot in the end. Working from the wrong side to the right, embroider the eyes, cheeks, nose, and mouth in satin stitch (see page 111).

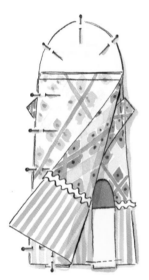

7. Lay the front of the doll on your work surface. Pin and baste (tack) the arms and legs onto it, positioning the arms at a slight downward angle. With right sides together, pin and machine stitch the front to the back, leaving the bottom open. Make small snips in the seam allowance around the head. Turn the doll right side out and press.

8. Turn the doll wrong side out again. With right sides together, pin and machine stitch the base in place, leaving a gap of about 3 in. (7 cm). Turn right side out. Fill the body about two thirds full with polyester toy filling or kapok, then fill the remaining space with dried peas or similar (see page 110). Whipstitch the gap closed (see page 111).

9. To make the hair, thread a tapestry needle with a long length of yarn. Stitch into the head, toward the right-hand side, bringing the needle back out of the head a short distance away. Cut the yarn to the length required and continue to stitch along the hairline to the back of the head. Trim the hair into a neat bob. To finish, hand stitch a ribbon bow onto the head, two buttons onto the body, and a button onto each shoe.

Chapter Two

In the Garden

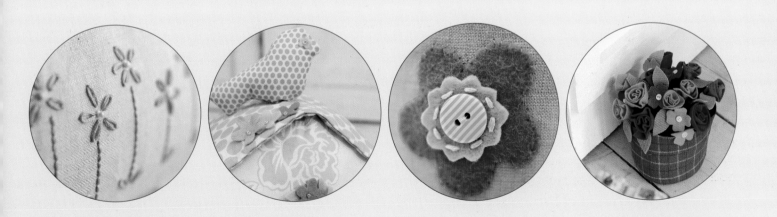

Birdhouse

Perfect for a conservatory door, this cute birdhouse doorstop will bring the outside indoors. Make birds from scraps of polka-dot fabric and stitch them securely onto the birdhouse, so that the bird on the roof can double up as a handle. Sweet little felt flowers add a touch of color, although these can be omitted if you wish.

You will need

Patterns on page 119

31½ x 29½ in. (80 x 75 cm) medium-weight iron-on interfacing

27½ x 20 in. (70 x 50 cm) patterned fabric

27½ x 8 in. (70 x 20 cm) polka-dot fabric

3¼-in. (8-cm) square of fusible bonding web

3¼-in. (8-cm) square of coordinating fabric

Polyester toy filling or kapok

Dried peas or similar

12 x 4 in. (30 x 10 cm) each of two fabrics for birds

2¾ x 1½ in. (7 x 4 cm) felt in three colors

Embroidery floss (thread)

2¼ x 2 in. (5.5 x 5 cm) brown polka-dot fabric for perch

2½ x 1½ in. (6 x 4 cm) green felt

Take ⅜-in. (1-cm) seam allowances throughout, unless otherwise stated.

1. Following the manufacturer's instructions, apply interfacing to the wrong side of the patterned and polka-dot fabrics. Enlarge the patterns on page 119 to twice the size and cut out. Cut one front, one back, two sides, one base, and two roof pieces from the patterned fabric. Cut four 6⅛ x 6⅝-in. (15.5 x 16.5-cm) pieces of polka-dot fabric for the tiled roof pieces.

2. Following the manufacturer's instructions, apply fusible bonding web to the wrong side of the coordinating fabric. Draw a circle 2⅝ in. (6.5 cm) in diameter on the paper side. Cut it out and peel off the backing paper. Position the circle on one of the front pieces, centered on the width and 3¼ in. (8 cm) from the bottom edge. Cover with a damp cloth and press with a warm iron to stick the circle in place. Machine stitch around the edge.

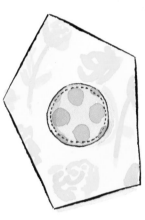

3. Pin and machine stitch one roof piece to a side piece. Repeat with the second roof and side pieces, then pin and stitch the two roof pieces together to make one long strip. Press all the seams open.

4. With right sides together, aligning the bottom edges, pin and machine stitch the strip to the front piece along the sides and the roof. Make a snip at each corner in the seam allowance and press the seam open.

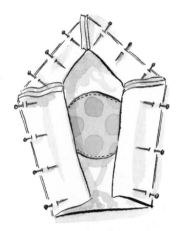

5. Pin and stitch the back to the sides in the same way. Make snips in the seam allowance again, turn right side out, and press.

6. With right sides together, pin and machine stitch two of the spotted roof pieces together along their short edges. Press the seam open. Repeat with the two remaining polka-dot roof pieces.

7. With right sides together, pin and machine stitch the two pairs of roof pieces together, leaving a 3-in. (8-cm) gap along one long side. Cut the corners of the seam allowance off, turn right side out, and press. Whipstitch the gap closed (see page 111).

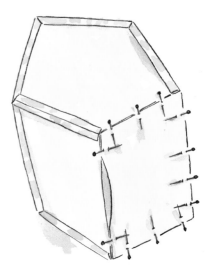

8. Pin and baste (tack) the roof to the top of the house, and machine stitch in place, sewing along the inside seams of the top of the house. Remove the basting (tacking) stitches. Press the seam open.

9. Turn the birdhouse wrong side out. With right sides together, aligning the corners of the base with the seams of the birdhouse, pin the base in place. Machine stitch, starting and finishing ⅜ in. (1 cm) from the edges, making a snip at each corner as you sew and leaving a 3-in. (8-cm) gap along the back edge. Turn the birdhouse right side out and press.

10. Fill the birdhouse about two thirds full with polyester toy filling or kapok, then fill the remaining space with dried peas or similar (see page 110). Whipstitch the gap in the base closed).

11. Using the pattern on page 119, cut two bird shapes from one of the bird fabrics. Cut out two small felt flowers and stitch one onto each bird shape to make the eyes, sewing a French knot (see page 111) in the center to fix them in place. With right sides together, pin and machine stitch the two bird shapes together, leaving a 1¼-in. (3-cm) gap along the top edge. Cut the corners of the seam allowance off, turn the bird right side out, and press. Stuff the bird with polyester toy filling, then whipstitch the opening closed. Repeat with the second bird fabric.

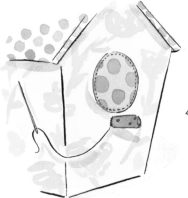

12. Fold the brown polka-dot fabric for the perch in half, right sides together, and machine stitch along the long raw edge and one short end. Cut the corner off and turn the perch right side out. Press, turning the raw end to the wrong side by ⅜ in. (1 cm). Push a small piece of polyester toy filling inside and whipstitch the open end of the perch onto the front of the house, just under the fabric circle.

13. Whipstitch the birds onto the house, stitching one onto the perch and one onto the roof. Using the patterns on page 119, cut two large flower shapes from each of the three colored felts and three green leaves. Put a leaf behind three of the flowers and stitch them onto the front of the house, using a French knot in the center of the flower to secure them. Stitch the remaining flowers onto the roof in the same way to finish.

Embroidered doorstop

Don't worry if your embroidery skills are very basic. This doorstop is simple to make and doesn't require any great knowledge of different stitches. Embroidery flosses (threads) come in a wonderful selection of colors. Choose colors that you like and put them together with your fabric to make a pleasing combination.

You will need

40 x 20 in. (100 x 50 cm) medium-weight iron-on interfacing

40 x 20 in. (100 x 50 cm) solid-color fabric

Fadeaway fabric marker pen

Embroidery floss (thread) in green, yellow, and three shades of pink

Two buttons, approx. ¾ in. (2 cm) in diameter

Polyester toy filling or kapok

Dried peas or similar

Take ⅜-in. (1-cm) seam allowances throughout, unless otherwise stated.

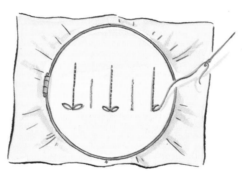

1. Following the manufacturer's instructions, apply interfacing to the wrong side of the fabric. Cut three pieces of fabric about 12 in. (30 cm) square and place one in an embroidery hoop. Using a fadeaway fabric marker pen, draw five straight lines for the stalks 1 in. (2.5 cm) apart, making the outer and central lines about 1¾ in. (4.5 cm) long and the other two about 1 in. (2.5 cm) long.

2. Thread an embroidery needle with green floss (thread) and tie a knot in the end. Work small, neat backstitches down the left-hand line, ending with a lazy daisy stitch (see page 111) on either side at the bottom of the stalk for the leaves. Repeat for the remaining stalks, stitching either one or two leaves at the bottom of each stalk.

3. Using the pink flosses (threads), work five lazy daisy stitches at the top of each stalk to make the flowers. Work a yellow French knot (see page 111) at the center of each flower. Remove the fabric from the hoop, lay a clean cloth on top, and press. Put the second piece of fabric in the hoop and embroider three flowers with stalks for one end of the doorstop. Repeat with the third piece of fabric for the other end of the doorstop.

4. Cut an 8¾ x 5½-in. (22 x 14-cm) rectangle and a 5½-in. (14-cm) square of paper. Lay the rectangle on the embroidered panel with five flowers, making sure that the embroidery is positioned centrally inside the rectangle and 1¼ in. (3 cm) from the bottom edge. Pin the paper in place and cut out. Cut another three rectangles of plain fabric using the paper pattern. Place the paper square over the panels with three flowers, as in the previous step, and cut out. These pieces will form the ends of the doorstop.

5. Cut a 7 x 3½-in. (18 x 8-cm) rectangle of fabric and make the handle, following method 1 on page 110. Pin and machine stitch the handle to one of the plain rectangles, positioning it 2 in. (5 cm) in from each short end and centered on the width. Stitch a cross at each end to make the handle strong. Sew a button onto the end of each side of the handle.

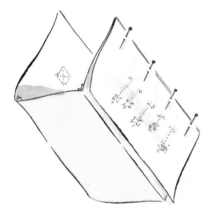 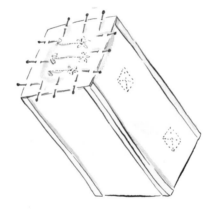

6. With right sides together, pin and machine stitch the rectangle with the handle to the top edge of the embroidered rectangle and press the seam open. Pin and machine stitch the other two plain fabric rectangles onto this to make an open-ended cube. Press the seams open.

7. With right sides together, pin one of the embroidered squares onto one end of the fabric cube, making sure that the embroidery is the right way up. Machine stitch in place, starting and finishing ⅜ in. (1 cm) in from the edge and making a small snip in each corner as you sew. Turn right side out and press.

8. Turn wrong side out again. Repeat step 7 to stitch the second end in place, leaving a 3-in. (7-cm) gap along the bottom edge. Turn right side out and press. Fill the top half of the block with polyester toy filling or kapok and the remaining space with dried peas or similar (see page 110). Whipstitch the gap closed (see page 111).

Felt flowers

A simple cylindrical shape is given extra detail with the addition of appliquéd felt flowers.

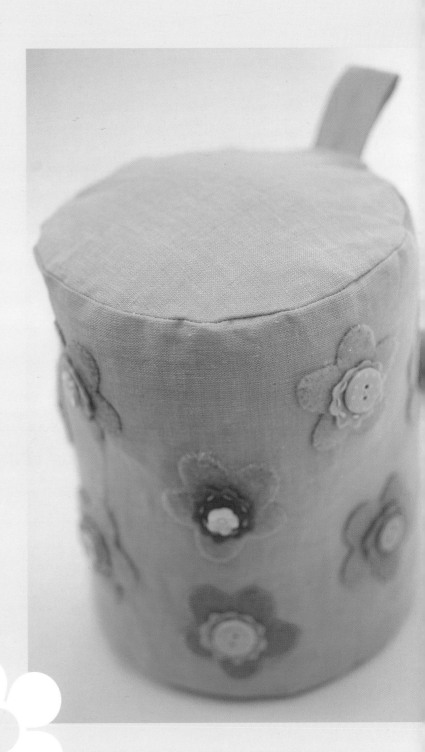

You will need

Patterns on page 120

40 x 10 in. (100 x 25 cm) medium-weight iron-on interfacing

40 x 10 in. (100 x 25 cm) solid-color fabric

Felt in coordinating colors

14 buttons, ⅜–⅝ in. (1–1.5 cm) in diameter

Embroidery floss (thread) in different colors

Polyester toy filling or kapok

Dried peas or similar

Take ⅜-in. (1-cm) seam allowances throughout, unless otherwise stated.

1. Following the manufacturer's instructions, apply interfacing to the wrong side of the fabric. Cut a 10⅛ x 8-in. (25.5 x 20-cm) rectangle of paper. Fold the fabric in half. Lay the paper rectangle on it, with one short side against the fold, and cut out. Cut a paper circle 6¾ in. (17 cm) in diameter for the ends and a strip measuring 4⅜ x 2¾ in. (11 x 7 cm) for the tab. Cut out two fabric circles and one tab.

2. Trace the patterns on page 120 at the size shown and cut out. Use these to cut out 14 flowers and 14 flower centers in different-colored felts.

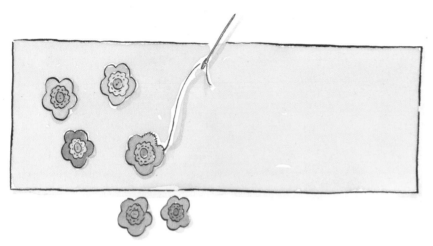 

3. Using embroidery floss (thread) and running stitch (see page 111), stitch the centers onto the flowers. Using regular sewing thread, sew a button to the center of each flower. Pin the flowers to the right side of the large rectangle, making sure that they are at least ¾ in. (2 cm) from the edges. Hand stitch the flowers in place with small straight stitches.

4. With right sides together, pin and machine stitch the two short edges of the rectangle together to form a tube. Press the seam open.

5. Fold the fabric for the tab in half lengthwise, right sides together. Pin and stitch along the long raw edge, turn right side out, and press. Fold the strip in half crosswise to make a loop. Aligning the raw edges, pin and baste (tack) it onto one of the end circles.

 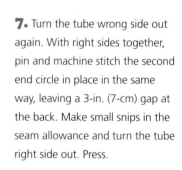

7. Turn the tube wrong side out again. With right sides together, pin and machine stitch the second end circle in place in the same way, leaving a 3-in. (7-cm) gap at the back. Make small snips in the seam allowance and turn the tube right side out. Press.

8. Fill the tube about two thirds full with polyester toy filling or kapok, then fill the remaining space with dried peas or similar (see page 110). Whipstitch the gap closed (see page 111).

6. With right sides together, pin and stitch the end onto one end of the fabric tube, aligning the tab with the seam of the tube. Make small snips in the seam allowance (see page 109), turn the tube right side out, and press.

Pear

This charming doorstop is so simple to make and has a pleasingly plump shape. Checked wool fabrics give it a very classic feel, but you could try velvets for a more sumptuous look or brightly patterned cotton fabrics for a child's room.

You will need

Patterns on page 120

Two 20 x 14-in. (50 x 35-cm) pieces of medium-weight iron-on interfacing

20 x 14 in. (50 x 35 cm) each of two tweed fabrics

6½-in. (16-cm) square of green wool fabric

3⅓ x 1⅜ in. (8 x 3.5 cm) brown wool fabric

Polyester toy filling or kapok

Dried peas or similar

Take ⅜-in. (1-cm) seam allowances throughout, unless otherwise stated.

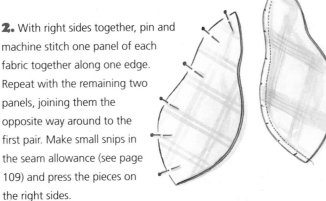

1. Following the manufacturer's instructions, apply interfacing to the wrong side of the tweed fabrics. Enlarge the patterns on page 120 to twice the size and cut out. Laying the pattern diagonally across the fabric, so that the check will be at an angle, cut two pear panels from each tweed fabric.

2. With right sides together, pin and machine stitch one panel of each fabric together along one edge. Repeat with the remaining two panels, joining them the opposite way around to the first pair. Make small snips in the seam allowance (see page 109) and press the pieces on the right sides.

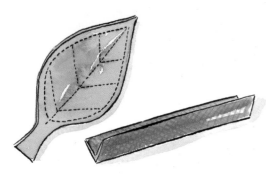

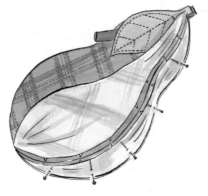

3. Cut two leaf shapes from the green fabric. Pin them together and machine stitch the veins, then stitch all around, as close as possible to the edge. Take the piece of brown fabric for the stem, fold over ⅜ in. (1 cm) to the wrong side along one long edge, then fold the other long edge over to meet the fold. Machine stitch along its length.

4. Pin and baste (tack) the stem and leaf onto the right side of one pear half. With right sides together, pin and machine stitch the two pear halves together, leaving a 3-in. (8-cm) gap at the bottom. Make small snips in the seam allowance all around the pear and turn right side out. Press.

5. Fill the pear about two thirds full with polyester toy filling or kapok, then fill the remaining space with dried peas or similar (see page 110). Whipstitch the gap closed (see page 111).

Toadstool

I love the combination of red polka-dot fabric and natural linen, and they work really well together in this delightful toadstool doorstop. The chunky stem forms a nice solid base, with small pearly buttons adding an extra decorative touch. The buttons can, of course, be left off if you are making this for a small child.

You will need

Pattern on page 120

30 x 16 in. (75 x 40 cm) natural linen

42 x 16 in. (105 x 40 cm) medium-weight iron-on interfacing

12-in. (30-cm) square of red polka-dot fabric

Polyester toy filling or kapok

Dried peas or similar

11 odd buttons approx. ⅜ in. (1 cm) in diameter

Take ⅜-in. (1-cm) seam allowances throughout, unless otherwise stated.

1. Cut a 15 x 3¼-in. (38 x 8-cm) rectangle of natural linen. Machine stitch along one long side, 1¼ in. (3 cm) from the edge.

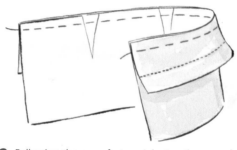

2. Following the manufacturer's instructions, apply interfacing to the wrong side of the remaining linen and polka-dot fabrics. Enlarge the pattern on page 120 to twice the size—it should be a 15 x 6-in. (38 x 15-cm) rectangle. Cut it from the interfaced linen. With right sides together, lay the rectangle from step 1 on top of this, with the stitch line toward the bottom. Pin and baste (tack) along the top edge. Mark the positions of the darts on the wrong side. Pin and machine stitch the darts through both layers. Press.

3. Fold the rectangle in half lengthwise, right sides together. Pin and machine stitch the two short sides together to make the stalk. Press the seam open. Cut a circle of linen 4⅜ in. (11 cm) in diameter and one 5⅛ in. (13 cm) in diameter. With right sides together, pin and machine stitch the smaller circle to the top of the stalk. Cut small snips in the seam allowance (see page 109) and press. Turn right side out.

4. For the underside of the toadstool, cut a 27¼ x 4¾-in. (69 x 12-cm) rectangle of linen. With right sides together, pin and machine stitch the short edges together and press the seam open. Work a line of running stitch along one edge and pull the thread to gather. Secure with a few small stitches.

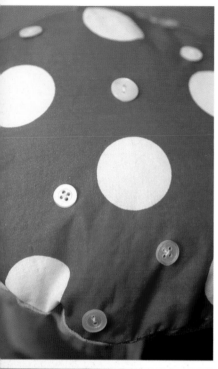

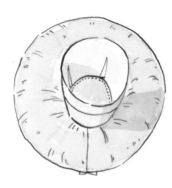

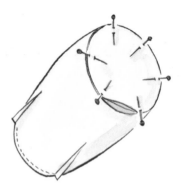

5. With right sides together, aligning the seams, pin and machine stitch the top of the stalk to the center of the underside of the toadstool.

6. Turn the stalk wrong side out, tucking the underside of the toadstool inside it. With right sides together, pin and machine stitch the larger circle from step 3 to the bottom of the stalk, leaving a gap of about 3 in. (8 cm) near the seam. Make small snips in the seam allowance and turn the stalk right side out. Press.

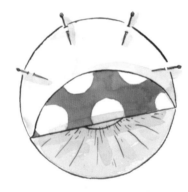

7. Cut a circle of polka-dot fabric 9¼ in. (23.5 cm) in diameter. With right sides together, pin and machine stitch the circle to the underside of the toadstool, leaving a gap of about 3 in. (8 cm) near the seam of the underside. Make small snips in the seam allowance, turn right side out, and press.

8. Push polyester toy filling or kapok inside the top of the toadstool to make a plump, even shape. Whipstitch the gap closed (see page 111). Fill the stalk about two thirds full with toy filling or kapok, then fill the remaining space with dried peas or similar (see page 110). Whipstitch the gap closed.

9. Sew buttons onto the top of the toadstool between the dots on the polka-dot fabric. Make snips about ¼ in. (5 mm) apart and 1 in. (2.5 cm) deep to make the frill, taking care not to cut through the stitch line from step 1.

Flowerpot

A great gift for a gardener, this cute flowerpot doorstop will be much admired. Choose fabrics that will not fray for the flowers—felted wool is perfect. Make as many flowers as you like, pinning them onto the pot until you are happy with the arrangement and then stitching them firmly in place.

You will need

Patterns on page 121

32 x 18 in. (80 x 45 cm) checked wool fabric

22 x 6 in. (55 x 15 cm) fusible bonding web

22 x 18 in. (55 x 45 cm) medium-weight iron-on interfacing

10-in. (25-cm) square of brown felt

Polyester toy filling or kapok

Dried peas or similar

Wool fabrics in shades of pink and red for roses

Green wool fabric for leaves

Selection of small buttons

Take ⅜-in. (1-cm) seam allowances throughout, unless otherwise stated.

1. Cut a 22 x 6-in. (55 x 15-cm) piece of checked wool fabric. Following the manufacturer's instructions, apply fusible bonding web to the wrong side. Apply interfacing to the wrong side of the remaining checked fabric.

2. Enlarge the patterns on page 121 to twice the size and cut out. Cut a pot and a base from the interfaced fabric and a rim from the piece of fabric with fusible bonding web.

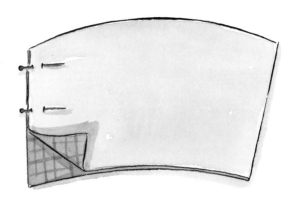

3. With right sides together, pin and machine stitch the two short edges of the pot together. Press the seam open.

4. Cut a circle of brown felt 9 in. (23 cm) in diameter. Work a line of running stitch (see page 111) around the edge and gather it slightly. With right sides together, push the felt circle inside the top of the pot and arrange it so that it fits snugly. Pin and machine stitch the felt to the pot. Make small snips in the seam allowance.

5. With right sides together, pin and machine stitch the base to the bottom of the pot, leaving a gap of about 3 in. (7 cm) along the back near the seam. Make small snips along the seam allowance (see page 109) and turn the pot right side out. Press.

6. Take the checked fabric rim and peel the backing paper off the fusible bonding web. Pin and machine stitch the short edges together and press the seam open. Slip the rim over the top edge of the pot, making sure that the seam of the rim lines up with the seam of the pot. Place a damp cloth over the top, and press with a warm iron to stick the rim in place.

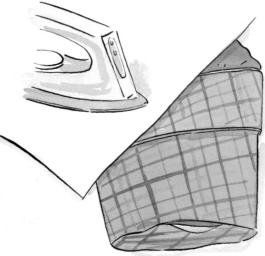

7. Fill the pot about two thirds full with polyester toy filling or kapok, then fill the remaining space with dried peas or similar (see page 110). Whipstitch the gap closed (see page 111).

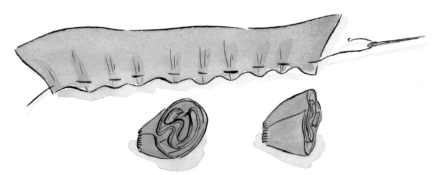

8. Measure and cut about 14 strips of the pink and red wool fabric measuring 16 x 1¼ in. (40 x 3 cm). Work a line of running stitch along the bottom edge of each strip, pull the thread to gather slightly, and secure with a few small stitches. Coil the strips into a rose shape and stitch through all the layers to secure.

9. Using the patterns on page 121, cut a flower shape and a leaf shape from paper. Use these to cut 12 flowers from pink and red wool fabrics and 14 leaf shapes from green wool fabric.

10. Pin the roses randomly onto the brown felt and hand stitch them in place. Arrange the leaves around the coiled roses and stitch one end of each onto the brown felt. Sew the flat flowers between the roses, stitching a button at the center of each one.

Woodland garden

Felt funghi decorate this charming woodland-inspired doorstop. Use striped and polka-dot fabrics in shades of green for the basic hill shape and have fun making toadstool and leaf decorations.

1. Following the manufacturer's instructions, apply interfacing to the wrong side of the polka-dot and striped fabrics. Enlarge the patterns on page 121 to twice the size and cut out. Cut three hill sections from each fabric and one base from the striped fabric.

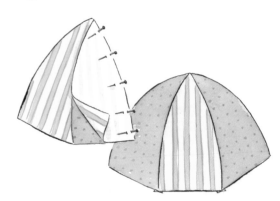

2. With right sides together, pin and machine stitch a striped section to a polka-dot section. Pin and machine stitch another striped section to the other edge of the polka-dot one, snip the seam allowances (see page 109), and press the seams open. Repeat using the three remaining sections, this time sewing a polka-dot section to either side of the striped one.

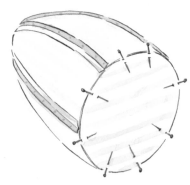

3. With right sides together, pin and machine stitch the two halves together, leaving the bottom edge open. Make small snips in the seam allowance and press the seams open.

4. With right sides together, pin and machine stitch the base in place, leaving a gap of about 3 in. (8 cm). Cut small snips in the seam allowance all the way around, turn the hill right side out, and press.

5. Fill the hill about two thirds full with polyester toy filling or kapok, then fill the remaining space with dried peas or similar (see page 110). Whipstitch the gap closed (see page 111).

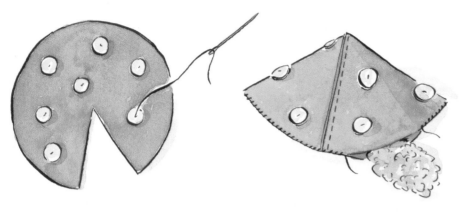

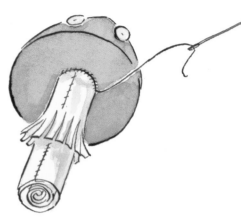

6. Now make the light brown toadstool. Using the pattern on page 121, cut a top and an underside from light brown felt. Cut a 4 x ¾-in. (10 x 2-cm) stalk, a 2½ x 1-in. (4 x 2.5-cm) frill, and seven spots from cream felt. Stitch the spots onto the top section, keeping the spots at least ¼ in. (5 mm) from the edges.

7. Overlap the two straight edges of the top to make a cone shape. Work a line of running stitch (see page 111) along the join, starting and finishing with a few small stitches. With wrong sides together, hand stitch the underside to the bottom of the cone shape, pushing a small piece of toy filling or kapok inside before you finish sewing.

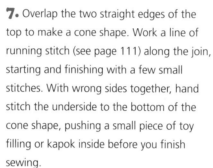

8. Roll up the cream felt stalk and whipstitch along the join. Cut snips all the way along the bottom of the frill section and stitch the frill around the top of the stalk. Hand stitch the stalk to the center of the underside of the toadstool top.

9. For the red and dark brown toadstools, using the pattern on page 121, cut a top and a bottom cap section for each from colored felt. Cut a 4 x 1⅜-in. (10 x 2.5-cm) stalk section and some spots in different sizes for each toadstool from white felt. Stitch the spots onto the top sections by working a few small stitches in the center of each. Whipstitch the top and bottom cap sections together, pushing toy filling inside before you finish. Sew the stalks in the same way as in step 8 and stitch to the underside of the tops.

10. Hand stitch the toadstools onto the hill by working small stitches around the bottom edge. Cut four large leaves and four small leaves from each shade of green felt and stitch them onto the hill in bunches of two or three by working a few small stitches at the base.

Chapter Three

Perfect Gifts

Cute cupcake

This pretty cupcake topped with a felt strawberry is the perfect doorstop for a little girl's bedroom. The decorative rick-rack edging, braids, and bead embellishments really make this project stand out.

Materials

Patterns on page 122

28 x 16 in. (70 x 40 cm) medium-weight iron-on interfacing

22 x 16 in. (55 x 40 cm) floral fabric for cup

Two 22-in. (55-cm) lengths of ribbon, one ⅝ in. (1.5 cm) and one ⅜ in. (1 cm) wide

22 in. (55 cm) rickrack braid, ⁵⁄₁₆ in. (8 mm) wide

8 x 8 in. (20 x 20 cm) white felt for frosting (icing)

12 x 12 in. (30 x 30 cm) gingham fabric for cake

Embroidery floss (thread) in pastel colors and yellow

Polyester toy filling or kapok

Dried lentils or similar

9 x 6 in. (22 x 15 cm) red felt and 6½ x 4 in. (16 x 10 cm) green felt for strawberry

Take ⅜-in. (1-cm) seam allowances throughout, unless otherwise stated.

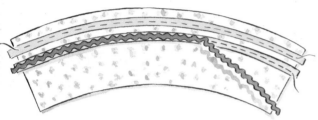

1. Following the manufacturer's instructions, apply interfacing to the wrong side of the cup fabric. Enlarge the patterns on page 122 to twice the size and cut out. Cut one side and one base from the cup fabric. Pin and stitch two lengths of ribbon around the top of the side piece, the first one about ¾ in. (2 cm) from the top edge and the second one about ⅜ in. (1 cm) from the first. Stitch rickrack braid along the center of the bottom ribbon.

2. With right sides together, pin and machine stitch the two short edges of the side piece together to form the cup shape. Press the seam open.

3. Using the pattern on page 122, cut a piece of white felt for the frosting (icing). Apply interfacing to the wrong side of the fabric for the cake and cut out a circle 11½ in. (29 cm) in diameter. Using white thread and small stitches, hand stitch the frosting onto the cake fabric. Decorate the frosting with French knots in pastel colors to look like sprinkles. Work a line of running stitch (see page 111) around the edge of the frosting, using a pastel-colored embroidery floss (thread).

4. With the cup inside out, pin and baste (tack) rickrack braid around the inside top edge, lining up the edge of the rickrack with the edge of the fabric. Work a line of running stitch around the edge of the cake circle and pull the thread slightly to gather it, so that it will fit around the cup.

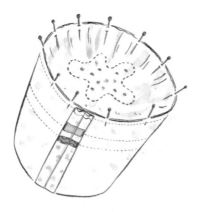

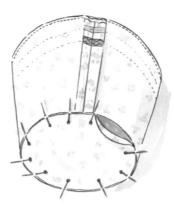

5. With right sides together, aligning the raw edges, pin, baste (tack), and then machine stitch the cake circle to the top of the cup. Turn right side out and press.

6. Turn the cup wrong side out again. With right sides together, pin and machine stitch the base to the bottom of the cup, leaving a gap of about 3 in. (8 cm). Make small snips around the seam allowance (see page 109) and turn the cup right side out. Press.

7. Fill the cake about two thirds full with polyester toy filling or kapok, then fill the remaining space with dried peas or similar (see page 110). Whipstitch the gap closed (see page 111).

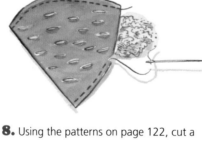

8. Using the patterns on page 122, cut a red felt strawberry, a green felt leaf, and a 3 x 1½-in. (8 x 4-cm) green felt stalk. Sew small yellow French knots randomly over the strawberry. With right sides together, fold the strawberry in half and machine stitch along the open sides, leaving a gap of 3 in. (8 cm). Turn right side out. Push in toy filling or kapok, then whipstitch the gap closed. Work running stitch around the top in red thread. Pull the thread to gather the strawberry and secure with a few small stitches.

9. Roll up the felt stalk and stitch along its length with green thread. Stitch the stalk to the leaf and then stitch the leaf onto the top of the strawberry. Stitch the strawberry onto the top of the cake, using small stitches to hold it securely in place.

Button cube

This project is a great way of using and displaying favorite buttons, and makes for a stylish and decorative doorstop. Combine brightly colored fabric with colorful buttons, as here, or natural linen with beautiful pearl buttons for a simple, elegant look.

You will need

28 x 16 in. (70 x 40 cm) medium-weight iron-on interfacing

28 x 16 in. (70 x 40 cm) solid-color fabric

Polyester toy filling or kapok

Dried peas or similar

20–25 buttons in different sizes

Take ⅜-in. (1-cm) seam allowances throughout, unless otherwise stated.

1. Following the manufacturer's instructions, apply interfacing to the wrong side of the fabric. Cut a 6½-in. (16-cm) paper square. Pin the paper onto the fabric and cut out six squares.

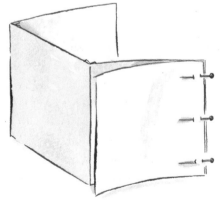

2. With right sides together, pin and machine stitch four squares together to form a row, then join the short ends of the row together to form an open-ended cube. Press the seams open.

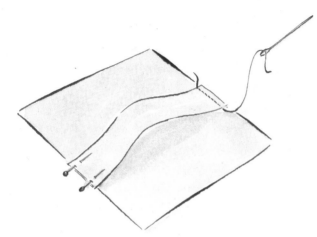

3. Cut an 8 x 3-in. (20 x 7-cm) rectangle of fabric and make the strap, following method 1 on page 110. Aligning the raw edges, pin and baste (tack) the strap across the middle of one of the two remaining squares.

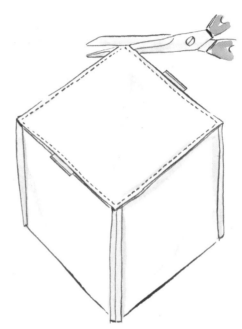

4. With right sides together, pin this square onto the top of the cube. Starting and finishing ⅜ in. (1 cm) from the edge, machine stitch along one side, then make a small diagonal snip at the corner. Continue around all four sides, making a small snip at each corner. Turn the cube right side out and press.

5. Turn the cube wrong side out again and repeat step 4 with the remaining square to form the base of the cube, leaving a 3-in. (8-cm) gap along one side. Turn the cube right side out and press.

6. Fill the cube two thirds full with polyester toy filling or kapok, then fill the rest of the space with dried peas or similar (see page 110). Whipstitch the gap closed (see page 111).

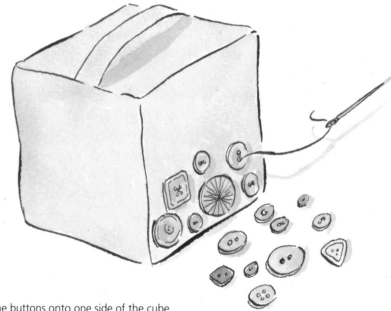

7. Stitch the buttons onto one side of the cube, playing around with the arrangement until you are happy with it. Use larger buttons toward the bottom and smaller ones at the top.

You will need

FOR ALL PYRAMIDS

Patterns on page 123

Polyester toy stuffing or kapok

Dried peas or similar

FOR LARGE PYRAMID

37 x 10½ in. (93 x 26 cm) medium-weight iron-on interfacing

10½ x 9 in. (26 x 23 cm) in each of two fabrics

27½ x 10½ in. (70 x 26 cm) contrasting fabric

4 in. (10 cm) ribbon, ¼ in. (5 mm) wide

FOR MEDIUM PYRAMID

32 x 9 in. (80 x 23 cm) medium-weight iron-on interfacing

8 x 7 in. (20 x 17 cm) in each of two fabrics

24 x 9 in. (60 x 23 cm) contrasting fabric

4 in. (10 cm) ribbon, ¼ in. (5 mm) wide

FOR SMALL PYRAMID

28½ x 8 in. (72 x 20 cm) medium-weight interfacing

8 x 7 in. (20 x 17 cm) in each of two fabrics

22 x 8 in. (55 x 20 cm) contrasting fabric

4 in. (10 cm) ribbon, ¼ in. (5 mm) wide

Take ⅜-in. (1-cm) seam allowances throughout, unless otherwise stated.

Pyramids

A useful loop makes these pyramid doorstops easier to grab and doubles as a hanger so that you can hang them on the door handle when not in use. The patterns on page 123 are for three different sizes—choose the larger one for a heavy door or one of the smaller ones for situations where a more lightweight doorstop is required.

1. Following the manufacturer's instructions, apply iron-on interfacing to the wrong side of the three fabrics for each size of pyramid. Enlarge the patterns on page 123 to twice the size and cut out. For each pyramid, cut one triangle each from the two smaller pieces of fabric and two triangles and one base square from the larger piece.

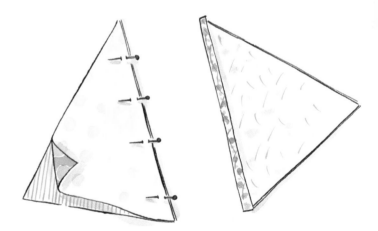

2. With right sides together, pin and machine stitch two of the triangles together along one long edge. Repeat with the second pair of triangles, making sure that each triangle will be next to one of a different fabric. Press the seams open.

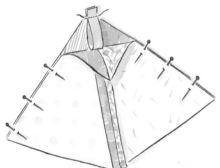

3. Take the ribbon and fold it into a loop. Pin and baste (tack) the unfolded ends to the right side of one of the pyramid halves at the top. With right sides together, pin and machine stitch the two pyramid halves together, leaving the base open. Double stitch across the ribbon so that it is held securely in place. Press the seams open, turn the pyramid right side out, and press.

4. Turn the pyramid wrong side out again. With right sides together, pin and machine stitch the pyramid to the base, starting and finishing ⅜ in. (1 cm) in from the edge and leaving a gap of about 3 in. (8 cm) along one side. Make a small snip in each corner as you go.

5. Turn the pyramid right side out and press. Fill the pyramid about half full with polyester toy filling or kapok, then fill the remaining space with dried peas or similar (see page 110). Whipstitch the gap closed (see page 111).

Rocket

You'll be over the moon when you make this delightful space-rocket doorstop. You can have great fun inventing your own decorations for it. Why not stitch a small face peering out of one of the windows, or the name of the owner to personalize it?

You will need

Patterns on page 123

24 x 20 in. (60 x 50 cm) medium-weight iron-on interfacing

24 x 20 in. (60 x 50 cm) wool fabric

16 in. (40 cm) gingham ribbon, ⅜ in. (1 cm) wide

16 in. (40 cm) gingham ribbon, ⅝ in. (1.5 cm) wide

9½-in. (24-cm) square of gray felt and matching thread

9½-in. (24-cm) square of blue felt and matching thread

Pale blue and pale green embroidery floss (thread)

2 x 1½ in. (5 x 4 cm) turquoise felt and matching thread

Two buttons, approx. ⅝ in. (1.5 cm) in diameter

Polyester toy filling or kapok

Dried peas or similar

Take ⅜-in. (1-cm) seam allowances throughout, unless otherwise stated.

1. Following the manufacturer's instructions, apply interfacing to the wrong side of the wool fabric. Enlarge the patterns on page 123 to twice the size and cut out. Cut four side pieces, one base, and eight fin pieces from the wool fabric.

2. With right sides together, pin and machine stitch two of the fin pieces together. Trim the seam allowance at the corner and turn right side out. Press. Repeat with the remaining fin pieces to make four fins in total.

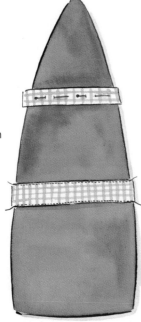

3. Cut each of the two ribbons into four equal lengths. Pin and topstitch them onto the side pieces, stitching along both edges of the ribbons. Trim the ends of the ribbons level with the edges of the rocket pieces.

4. Draw a circle 2 in. (5 cm) in diameter and another one 1¼ in. (3 cm) in diameter on paper and cut out. Pin the large circle to gray felt and the small circle to blue felt and cut four circles in each color.

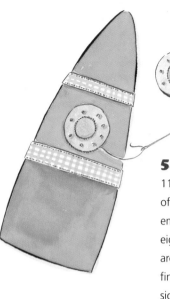

5. Pin and whipstitch (see page 111) each blue circle to the center of a gray circle. Using pale blue embroidery floss (thread), work eight French knots (see page 111) around the blue circle, starting and finishing with a knot on the wrong side. Whipstitch the circles onto the side pieces, positioning them between the ribbons.

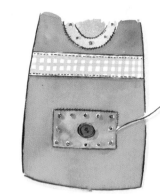

6. Cut two 1½ x 1-in. (4 x 2.5-cm) pieces of turquoise felt. Sew a button onto the center of each one and work 12 French knots around the edge in pale green embroidery floss (thread). Whipstitch the pieces onto two of the side pieces, centered on the width and about 2 in. (5 cm) below the bottom ribbon.

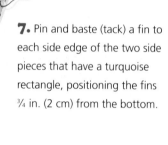

7. Pin and baste (tack) a fin to each side edge of the two side pieces that have a turquoise rectangle, positioning the fins ¾ in. (2 cm) from the bottom.

8. With right sides together, pin and machine stitch one of the remaining side pieces to a side piece with fins, stitching along the left-hand side. Make a few small snips in the seam allowance (see page 109). Repeat with the other two side pieces. Press the seams open.

9. With right sides together, pin and machine stitch the two rocket halves together, leaving the bottom edge open. Make a few small snips in the seam allowance. Press the seams open. Turn the rocket right side out and press it on the right side.

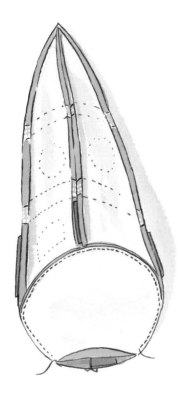

10. Turn the rocket wrong side out again. With right sides together, pin and machine stitch the base to the bottom of the rocket, leaving a gap of about 2½ in. (6 cm) in one side. Press. Turn right side out.

11. Fill the rocket about two thirds full with polyester toy filling or kapok, then fill the remaining space with dried peas or similar (see page 110). Whipstitch the gap closed.

Brick block

The success of this simple doorstop lies in the fabric choice. Use vintage fabric with a retro feel or choose brightly patterned designs. The handy loop means that the doorstop can be hung on a hook by the door or looped onto the door handle to move it out of the way when necessary.

You will need

31½ x 14 in. (80 x 35 cm) medium-weight iron-on interfacing

31½ x 14 in. (80 x 35 cm) fabric

Polyester toy filling or kapok

Dried peas or similar

Take ⅜-in. (1-cm) seam allowances throughout, unless otherwise stated.

1. Following the manufacturer's instructions, apply interfacing to the wrong side of the fabric. Cut pieces of paper measuring 10 x 5½ in. (25 x 14 cm) and 10 x 5 in. (25 x 13 cm) for the sides of the block and 5½ x 5 in. (14 x 13 cm) for the ends. Use them as patterns to cut two sides in each size and two end pieces from the fabric.

2. With right sides together, pin and machine stitch a larger side to a smaller side along one long side. Press the seam open. Repeat with the remaining two sides. Pin and machine stitch the two pairs of sides together to make an open-ended shape. Press the seams open and turn right side out.

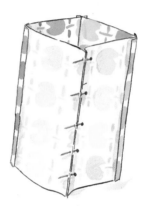

3. To make the loop, cut two strips of fabric measuring 4¾ x 2 in. (12 x 5 cm). With right sides together, pin and stitch the strips together along their long edges, leaving the short ends open. Turn right side out and press.

4. Fold the strip in half to make a loop. Aligning the raw edges, pin and baste (tack) it onto one of the short sides of one of the larger rectangles, centering it on the width.

5. Turn the shape wrong side out. With right sides together, pin and machine stitch one of the end pieces onto one end of the shape, aligning the corners of the end piece with the seams. Start and finish sewing ⅜ in. (1 cm) from the edges and make small snips in the corners as you sew.

6. Attach the other end piece to the other end of the shape in the same way, leaving a gap of about 3 in. (8 cm) along the bottom edge. Turn right side out and press. Fill the block about two thirds full with polyester toy filling or kapok, then fill the remaining space with dried peas or similar (see page 110). Whipstitch the gap closed (see page 111).

Block with handle

Choose two coordinating fabrics to make this simple block doorstop, adding ribbon to embellish it. Make use of scraps left over from soft furnishings to match the color scheme of the room, or add an extra splash of color to your decor with bold, contemporary patterns.

You will need

34 x 22 in. (85 x 55 cm) medium-weight iron-on interfacing

32 x 8 in. (80 x 20 cm) main fabric

24 x 12 in. (60 x 30 cm) coordinating fabric

24 in. (60 cm) velvet ribbon, ⅜ in. (1 cm) wide

Polyester toy filling or kapok

Dried peas or similar

Take ⅜-in. (1-cm) seam allowances throughout, unless otherwise stated.

1. Following the manufacturer's instructions, apply interfacing to the wrong side of both pieces of fabric. Cut a 25¾ x 5-in. (64 x 13-cm) strip and an 8 x 6-in. (20 x 15-cm) rectangle for the base of the block from the main fabric. Cut a 25¾ x 2⅜-in. (64 x 6-cm) strip and an 8 x 6-in. (20 x 15-cm) rectangle for the top of the block from the coordinating fabric.

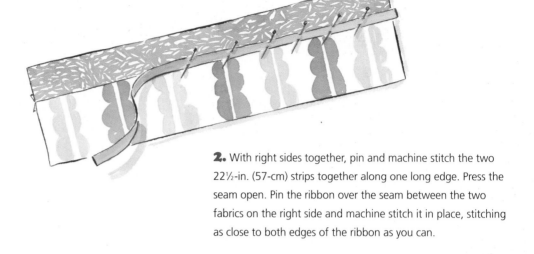

2. With right sides together, pin and machine stitch the two 22½-in. (57-cm) strips together along one long edge. Press the seam open. Pin the ribbon over the seam between the two fabrics on the right side and machine stitch it in place, stitching as close to both edges of the ribbon as you can.

3. With right sides together, pin and machine stitch the short sides of the panel together to form a loop. Press the seam open.

4. Cut two 10 x 2-in. (25 x 5-cm) strips of fabric from the coordinating fabric and make the handle, following method 2 on page 110. Pin and baste (tack) the handle centrally to the rectangle of fabric for the top of the block, aligning the raw edges.

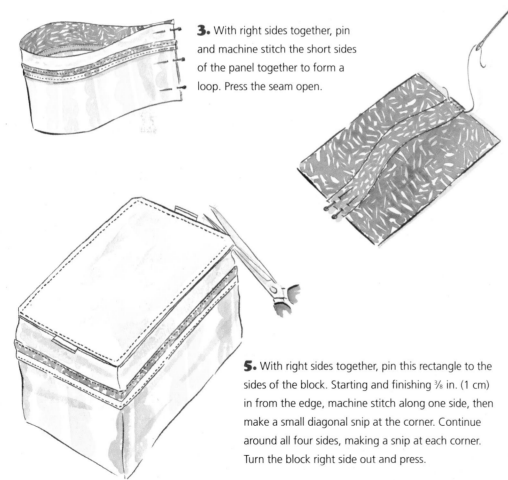

6. Turn wrong side out again. Repeat step 5 to stitch the base in place, leaving a 3-in. (8-cm) gap along one side. Turn right side out and press. Fill the block two thirds full with polyester toy filling or kapok, then fill the remaining space with dried peas or similar (see page 110). Whipstitch the gap closed (see page 111).

5. With right sides together, pin this rectangle to the sides of the block. Starting and finishing ⅜ in. (1 cm) in from the edge, machine stitch along one side, then make a small diagonal snip at the corner. Continue around all four sides, making a snip at each corner. Turn the block right side out and press.

Purse

This fun purse doorstop is perfect for a girl's bedroom door. Make a striking flower decoration like this one from muted wool fabrics or stitch on beads, shisha mirror, or sequins for a glitzy, glamorous alternative.

1. Following the manufacturer's instructions, apply interfacing to the wrong side of the wool fabric. Enlarge the patterns on page 124 to twice the size and cut out. Cut one front and one back panel, one gusset, one flap, and two handle pieces from the wool fabric. Cut one flap from the cotton fabric; this does not need interfacing.

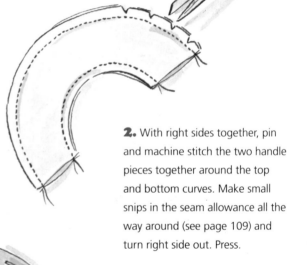

2. With right sides together, pin and machine stitch the two handle pieces together around the top and bottom curves. Make small snips in the seam allowance all the way around (see page 109) and turn right side out. Press.

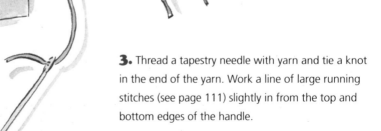

3. Thread a tapestry needle with yarn and tie a knot in the end of the yarn. Work a line of large running stitches (see page 111) slightly in from the top and bottom edges of the handle.

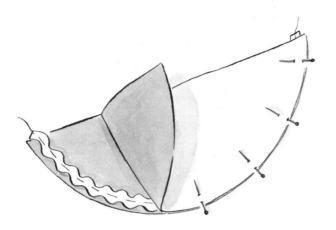

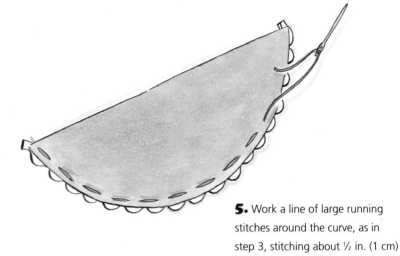

4. To make the flap, pin and baste (tack) the rickrack along the curved edge of the wool flap, ¼ in. (5 mm) (from the edge. With right sides together, pin and machine stitch the cotton flap to the wool one, stitching along the center of the rickrack and leaving the straight edge open. Make small snips around the seam allowance to form a nice curve. Turn right side out and press.

5. Work a line of large running stitches around the curve, as in step 3, stitching about ½ in. (1 cm) from the edge of the flap.

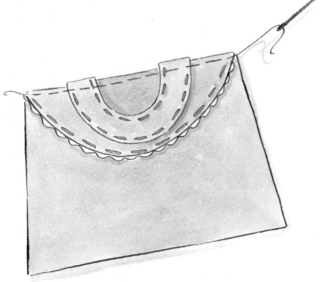

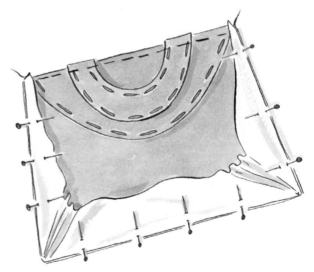

6. Lay one panel right side up on your work surface, with the flap right side up on top. Lay the handle centrally on top of the flap, aligning the raw edges. Baste (tack) through all the layers to hold them in place.

7. With right sides together, pin and machine stitch the gusset along one side of the panel, across the bottom, and up the other side, cutting diagonally across the seam allowance at the corners. Press on the right side.

8. Enlarge the flower patterns on page 124 to twice the size and cut out. Cut one large and one small flower from the squares of wool fabric. Stitch the smaller one onto the middle of the bigger one and sew a button onto the center. Stitch this onto the front of the purse, making sure that you stitch through all the layers to hold the flap in place as well.

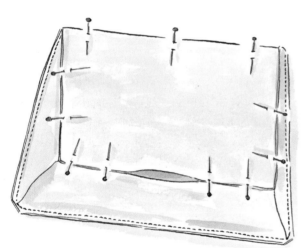

9. With right sides together, pin and machine stitch the second panel to the other side of the gusset, leaving a 3-in. (8-cm) gap along the bottom edge. Snip off the corners as before.

10. Turn the purse right side out and press. Fill the purse two thirds full with polyester toy filling or kapok, then fill the remaining space with dried peas or similar (see page 110). Whipstitch the gap closed (see page 111).

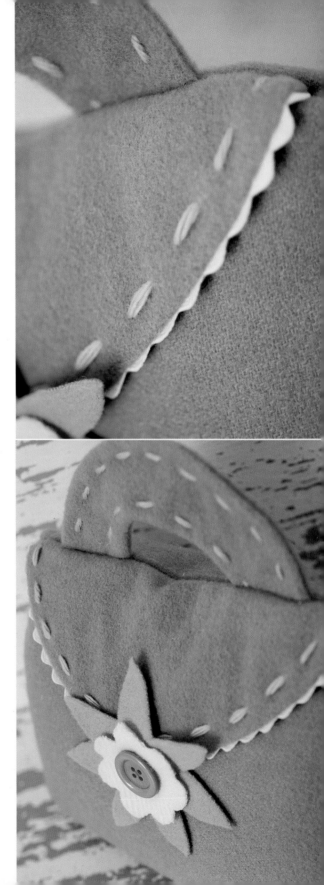

Velvet ball

For a stylishly opulent doorstop, make this simple ball shape with beautiful velvet fabrics. A button covered in velvet gives the doorstop a smart, sophisticated look, but a regular button would work just as well. Stitch a loop of ribbon between two of the segments to make a tab to carry and hang it.

You will need

Pattern on page 125

40 x 14 in. (100 x 35 cm) medium-weight iron-on interfacing

14 x 12 in. (35 x 30 cm) each of two colors of velvet

14 x 8 in. (35 x 20 cm) each of two colors of velvet

Polyester toy filling or kapok

Dried peas or similar

Self-covering button

Take ⅜-in. (1-cm) seam allowances throughout, unless otherwise stated.

1. Following the manufacturer's instructions, apply interfacing to the wrong side of the pieces of velvet. Enlarge the pattern on page 125 to twice the size and cut out. Cut two segments from each large piece of velvet and one segment from each small piece.

2. With right sides together, pin and machine stitch two different-colored segments together along one edge. Make small snips in the seam allowance (see page 109), turn right side out, and press. Pin and machine stitch a third segment to the other side of the first one, again making snips in the seam allowance. Press.

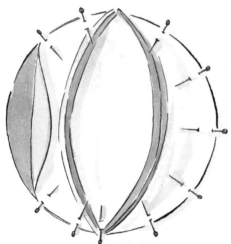

3. Stitch the remaining three segments together in the same way, making sure that each segment is next to one of a different color. With right sides together, pin and machine stitch the two halves together, leaving a gap of about 3 in. (8 cm) in one seam at the bottom. Snip around the seam allowances, turn right side out, and press.

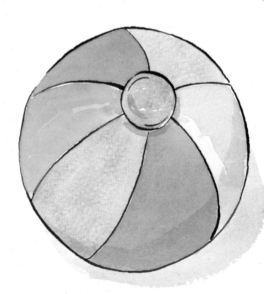

4. Fill the ball about two thirds full with polyester toy filling or kapok, then fill the remaining space with dried peas or similar (see page 110). Whipstitch the gap closed (see page 111). Following the manufacturer's instructions, cover the button with a piece of velvet. Hand stitch the button securely onto the top of the ball.

Tweed cube

The tailored look of this tweed fabric doorstop makes it perfect for a smart living room or study door. Stitch buttons onto four sides of the cube, leaving the bottom and back unadorned so that buttons will not scratch the door or floor.

You will need

Four 20 x 8 in. (50 x 20 cm) pieces of medium-weight iron-on interfacing

20 x 8 in. (50 x 20 cm) each of four different tweed fabrics

Polyester toy filling or kapok

Dried peas or similar

10–15 buttons, approx. ⅝ in. (1.5 cm) in diameter

Take ⅜-in. (1-cm) seam allowances throughout, unless otherwise stated.

1. Following the manufacturer's instructions, apply interfacing to the wrong side of all the fabric pieces. Cut a 7¼ x 2⅜-in. (18 x 6-cm) rectangle of paper to use as your pattern. Cut six rectangles from each fabric.

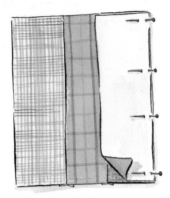

2. With right sides together, pin and machine stitch the rectangles of four different fabrics together along one long side to make a square. Press the seams open. Repeat with the remaining strips to make six squares.

3. To make the tab, cut two 5½ x 1¾-in. (14 x 4.5-cm) rectangles of one of the fabrics. With right sides together, pin and machine stitch them together along the long edges, leaving the short ends open. Turn right side out and press. Fold the tab in half lengthwise to form a loop. Aligning the raw edges, pin and baste (tack) the loop to the right side of one of the two remaining squares, centering it on the width.

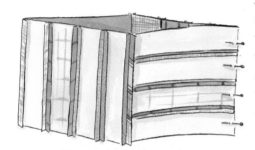

4. With right sides together, alternating the direction of the strips, pin and machine stitch four squares together to make a long strip. Press the seams open. With right sides together, pin and machine the short ends of the long strip together to form an open-ended cube. Press the seam open.

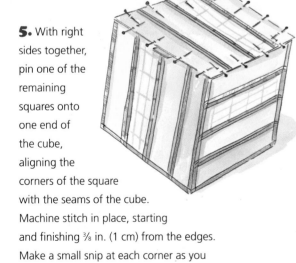

5. With right sides together, pin one of the remaining squares onto one end of the cube, aligning the corners of the square with the seams of the cube. Machine stitch in place, starting and finishing ⅜ in. (1 cm) from the edges. Make a small snip at each corner as you sew. Turn right side out and press.

6. Turn wrong side out again and pin and stitch the last square in place as in step 5, leaving a gap of about 3 in. (8 cm) along the bottom edge. Turn right side out and press. Fill the cube about two thirds full with polyester toy filling or kapok, then fill the remaining space with dried peas or similar (see page 110). Whipstitch the gap closed (see page 111).

7. Hand stitch two or three buttons onto the top and each side of the cube to finish.

Gathered bag

This simple, gathered doorstop is made from two coordinating fabrics. The outer bag can easily be taken off to launder.

You will need

24 x 16 in. (60 x 40 cm) canvas fabric

Polyester toy filling or kapok

Dried peas or similar

33½ x 16 in. (85 x 40 cm) main fabric

26 x 16 in. (65 x 40 cm) coordinating fabric

20 in. (50 cm) cord

Take ⅜-in. (1-cm) seam allowances throughout, unless otherwise stated.

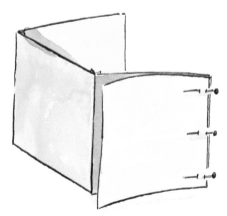

1. Cut six 6¾-in. (17-cm) squares of canvas fabric. With right sides together, pin and machine stitch two of the squares together along one edge. Press the seam open. Pin and stitch on two more squares, then join in a loop to form an open-ended cube. Press the seams open.

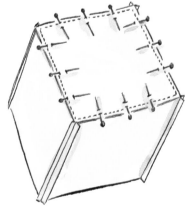

2. With right sides together, aligning the corners of the square with the seams of the cube, pin one of the two remaining squares onto one end of the cube. Starting and finishing ⅜ in. (1 cm) from the edge, machine stitch along one side, then make a small diagonal snip at the corner. Continue around all four sides, making a small snip at each corner. Press the seams open. Pin and stitch the last square to the other end of the cube in the same way, leaving a gap of about 3 in. (8 cm) along one side. Turn the cube right side out and press.

3. Fill the cube about two thirds full with polyester toy filling or kapok, then fill the remaining space with dried peas or similar (see page 110). Whipstitch the gap closed (see page 111).

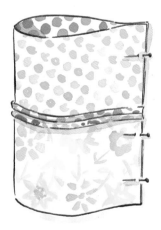

4. To make the outer bag, cut a piece of main fabric and coordinating fabric each measuring 24¾ x 14 in. (62 x 35 cm). Cut a 6¾-in. (17-cm) square from the main fabric for the base. With right sides together, pin and machine stitch the two rectangles of fabric together along one long side. Press the seam open. With right sides together, fold this panel in half and pin and machine stitch along the long raw edge. Press the seam open.

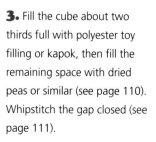

5. With right sides together, pin and machine stitch the base to the main fabric end of the shape, starting and finishing the stitching ³⁄₈ in. (1 cm) from the edge and making a small snip in the seam allowance at each corner as you sew. Press.

6. Turn the remaining raw edge to the wrong side by ¼ in. (5 mm) and then again by ³⁄₈ in. (1 cm). Press and topstitch to hem it. Turn right side out. Push the fabric inside the bag as far as it will go, so that the seam between the two fabrics forms the top edge, and press. Put the stuffed cube inside the bag, gather the fabric at the top, wrap the cord around, and tie in a secure knot. Finish by making a neat knot at each end of the cord and trim the cord ends.

You will need

Patterns on page 126

29½ x 16 in. (75 x 40 cm) medium-weight iron-on interfacing

29½ x 16 in. (75 x 40 cm) fabric

27½ in. (70 cm) white jumbo rickrack braid

27½ in. (70 cm) velvet ribbon, ¼ in. (5 mm) wide

4-in. (10-cm) square of brown felt

3⅝ x 1⅝ in. (9 x 4 cm) pink felt

16 in. (40 cm) white medium rickrack braid

Polyester toy filling or kapok

Dried peas or similar

8 x 7⅝ in. (20 x 19 cm) white felt

15 in. (38 cm) pink and green rickrack braid, ⁵⁄₁₆ in. (8 mm) wide

12 buttons, approx. ⅝ in. (1.5 cm) in diameter

Fast-drying hi-tack fabric glue

Take ⅜-in. (1-cm) seam allowances throughout, unless otherwise stated.

Gingerbread house

There are many doorstops in the shape of houses available to buy, but this gingerbread house is much more unusual. Use brown polka-dot fabric for the gingerbread, with rickrack braid for the frosting (icing). Pretty buttons in candy colors on the roof add a suitably sweet finishing touch.

1. Following the manufacturer's instructions, apply interfacing to the wrong side of the fabric. Enlarge the patterns on page 126 to twice the size and cut out. Cut two side pieces, one front, one back, two roof pieces, and one base.

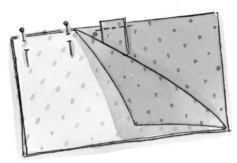

2. Cut a strip of fabric measuring 3⅝ x 2¾ in. (9 x 7 cm). Make a tab for the chimney, following method 1 on page 110. Fold the tab in half, with the seam on the inside. Aligning the raw edges, pin and baste (tack) it onto one long edge of one roof piece. Pin and machine stitch the second roof piece to the first, along the edge with the tab. Press the seam open.

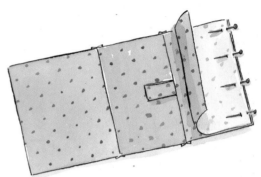

3. With right sides together, pin and machine stitch the front to one long raw edge of the roof. Press the seam open. Stitch the back to the other long raw edge of the roof and press the seam open.

4. With right sides together, pin and machine stitch the side panels to the front/roof/back section, matching the corners of the base with the seams of the house. Machine stitch in place, starting and finishing ⅜ in. (1 cm) from the edges and making a snip at each corner as you go. Turn right side out and press.

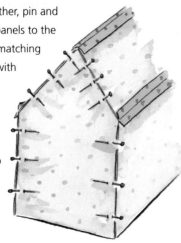

5. Pin and machine stitch the length of jumbo rickrack braid all around the right side of the house, ¾ in. (2 cm) from the bottom edge, overlapping the ends slightly and folding the top layer under at the back of the house. Pin and machine stitch the velvet ribbon just above the rickrack, again overlapping the ends and folding the top layer under.

6. Using the patterns on page 126, cut out paper patterns for the door, heart, and windows. Cut one door and two large windows from brown felt and two small windows and a heart from pink felt. Using small straight stitches, hand stitch the pink windows onto the brown windows and the heart to the door. Using running stitch (see page 111), hand stitch the white medium rickrack braid around the arch of the windows and the door, then stitch the windows and door onto the front of the house.

7. Turn the house wrong side out. With right sides together, aligning the corners of the base with the seams of the house, pin the base in place. Machine stitch, starting and finishing ⅜ in. (1 cm) from the edges, making a snip at each corner as you sew and leaving a 3-in. (7-cm) gap along the back edge. Turn the house right side out and press.

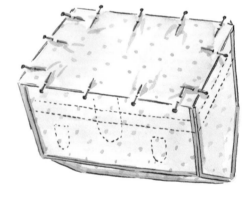

8. Fill the house about three-quarters full with polyester toy filling or kapok, then fill the remaining space with dried peas or similar (see page 110). Whipstitch the gap in the base closed (see page 111).

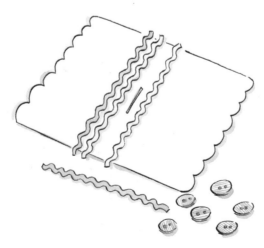

9. Using the pattern on page 126, cut a frosting (icing) roof from white felt. Cut a slit for the tab chimney where indicated. Cut the pink and green rickrack in half. Pin and machine stitch one strip of each color to the felt roof on either side of the slit, folding the ends neatly to the wrong side. Sew six buttons to each side of the felt roof. Apply glue to the roof of the house and slip the felt roof over the chimney. Hold in place until the glue is dry.

Chapter Four

Draft Excluders

Sweater draft excluder

Turn old sweaters that have seen better days into a cozy draft excluder—the perfect project if you are passionate about recycling. Add buttons for a stylish finishing touch.

1. Cut 14-in. (35-cm) strips from the sweaters, with the widths varying between 4 and 6¾ in. (10 and 17 cm). I cut two 6¾-in. (17-cm), one 6⅜-in. (16-cm), two 6-in. (15-cm), one 5¼-in. (13-cm), one 4¾-in. (12-cm), and one 4-in. (10-cm) strips.

2. Aligning the long edges, lay the strips out in a row, moving them around until you are happy with the arrangement. With right sides together, pin and machine stitch the strips together to form a panel. Press the seams open, using a cool iron.

❀ ❀ ❀ ❀ ❀ ❀ ❀ ❀ ❀ ❀

You will need

Old sweaters

Yarn in coordinating colors

Two self-covering buttons, approx. 1½ in. (4 cm) in diameter

Take ⅜-in. (1-cm) seam allowances throughout unless otherwise stated.

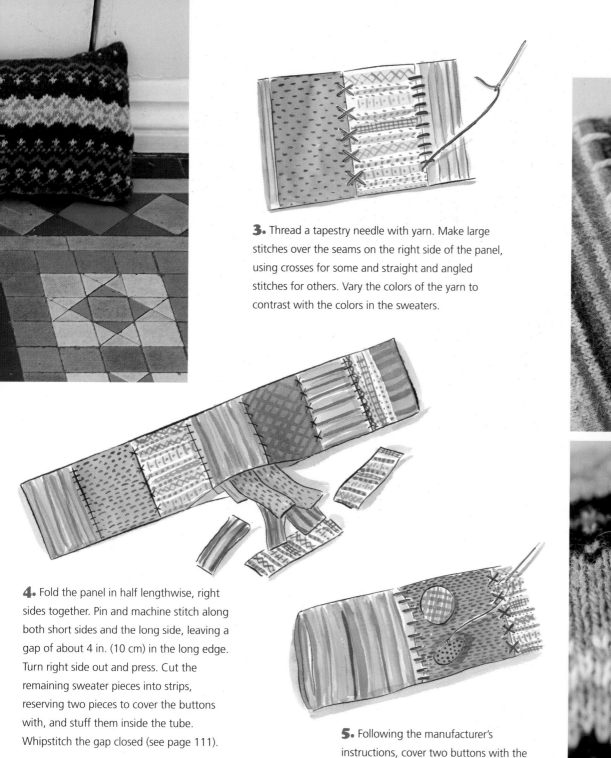

3. Thread a tapestry needle with yarn. Make large stitches over the seams on the right side of the panel, using crosses for some and straight and angled stitches for others. Vary the colors of the yarn to contrast with the colors in the sweaters.

4. Fold the panel in half lengthwise, right sides together. Pin and machine stitch along both short sides and the long side, leaving a gap of about 4 in. (10 cm) in the long edge. Turn right side out and press. Cut the remaining sweater pieces into strips, reserving two pieces to cover the buttons with, and stuff them inside the tube. Whipstitch the gap closed (see page 111).

5. Following the manufacturer's instructions, cover two buttons with the reserved pieces. Stitch the buttons onto the draft excluder to finish.

Yo-yo draft excluder

I love making fabric yo-yos. They look so pretty and this lovely draft excluder is the perfect opportunity to make lots of them! Use any remnants of fabric, or cut up old clothes that are too worn to pass on, mixing colors and patterns. If you can't get hold of big buttons, make smaller yo-yos for the ends and stitch a smaller button onto the middle of each. This one is about 32 in. (81 cm) long; for a wider door, simply add more yo-yos.

You will need

50 x 12-in. (30-cm) squares of fabric

Polyester toy filling or kapok

Approx. 100 in. (250 cm) yarn

Two buttons, approx. 1¾ in. (4.5 cm) in diameter

1. Draw a circle approx. 11 in. (28 cm) in diameter on paper and cut out. (Draw around a plate.) Pin the pattern to three fabric squares at a time and cut out. Repeat until you have 50 circles of fabric.

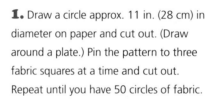

2. Thread a needle with sewing thread. Secure the thread to one of the fabric circles with a few small stitches and work a line of running stitch (see page 111) all around the circle, about ⅜ in. (1 cm) from the edge. Pull the thread to gather the fabric to make a yo-yo. Push small pieces of toy filling or kapok inside the yo-yo to pad it slightly, making sure it is evenly distributed. Pull the thread to close the center and secure with a few small stitches. Repeat with all the fabric circles.

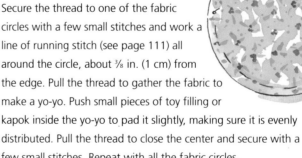

3. Thread a tapestry needle with a length of yarn and tie a knot in the end of the yarn. Stitch through a yo-yo from the back (the flat side) to the front (the gathered side). Thread the needle through the first button, then push the needle back through the button and the yo-yo.

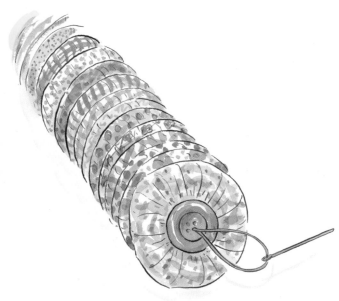

4. Stitch through each yo-yo to join them all together. At the other end, turn the last yo-yo over so that the gathered side is showing. Stitch though the other button. Take the needle and thread back through the button and all the yo-yos, and then back again to the other end of the draft excluder, so that the yo-yos are securely attached to each other. Finish with a knot on the back of the last yo-yo.

Tubular draft excluder

For a really quick and easy draft excluder, simply join panels of fabric together, stitch them into a tube, and stuff, adding a ribbon loop to make a handy hanger for when it is not in use. This one is 33 in. (84 cm) long. Simply increase the width of each of the fabric bands to make a draft excluder for a wider door.

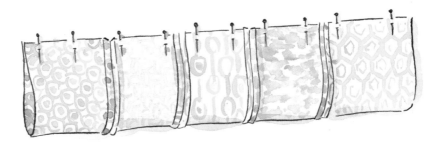

1. Arrange the five fabric rectangles in a row, with the larger pieces at either end. Pin and machine stitch them together along the long edge to form one long piece. Press the seams open. With right sides together, pin and machine stitch the two long edges together. Press the seam open.

2. Turn under ⅜ in. (1 cm) to the wrong side at each short end and press, then turn over another 1¼ in. (3 cm). Pin and machine stitch close to the inner folded edge to form a channel at each end, leaving a 1¼-in. (3-cm) gap. Turn right side out.

3. Cut a 6½-in. (16-cm) length of ribbon and fold it in half. Aligning the raw ends, pin the ribbon to the tube, then fold the ribbon back on itself, so that it sticks out above the tube, forming a loop. Stitch in place.

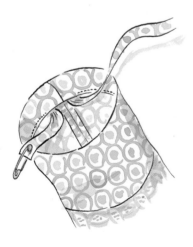

4. Cut the remaining ribbon in half. Fasten a safety pin to one end of one of the ribbon lengths and push it all the way through one of the channels. When it comes out the other side, remove the safety pin and pull the ribbon to gather the fabric. Secure with a knot and tie the ribbon in a bow to finish. Trim the ends of the ribbon neatly.

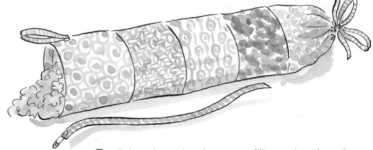

5. Fill the tube with polyester toy filling or kapok until it is nicely rounded (see page 110). Thread the other piece of ribbon through the other channel in the same way as before, again finishing with a neat bow.

Stripy draft excluder

This simple knitted draft excluder is quick to make and, as it uses only stockinette (stocking) stitch, requires only the most basic of knitting know-how. Buy balls of yarn specially or use up remnants left over from other projects to make a striking wooly draft excluder that will keep you warm and cozy. I've included a pattern for the draft excluder shown here, but you can make the stripes any size or color you wish.

You will need

1 x 2-oz (50-g) balls of Aran-weight wool each in mustard (M), blue (B), pink (P), green (G), and red (R)

One pair US size 8 (5 mm) knitting needles

34 x 6⅜ in. (86 x 16 cm) solid-color fabric

Compass and pencil

Cardstock

Tapestry needle

Polyester toy filling or kapok

Gauge (tension): 18 sts and 22 rows to 4 in. (10 cm) square over st st on US size 8 (5 mm) needles.

Take ⅜-in. (1-cm) seam allowances throughout, unless stated otherwise.

Knitting pattern

Using M and size 8 (5 mm) needles, cast on 30 stitches. Work 26 rows in st st.

Change to B and work 14 rows stitches in st st.

Change to P and work 14 rows in st st.

Change to G and work 24 rows in st st.

Change to R and work 6 rows in st st.

Change to B and work 6 rows in st st.

Change to M and work 16 rows in st st.

Change to P and work 12 rows in st st.

Change to R and work 10 rows in st st.

Change to B and work 4 rows in st st.

Change to G and work 12 rows in st st.

Change to M and work 12 rows in st st.

Change to P and work 6 rows in st st.

Change to B and work18 rows in st st.

Change to G and work 8 rows in st st.

Change to P and work 4 rows in st st.

Change to M, work 14 rows in st st, and bind (cast) off.

The finished length should be 34 in. (86 cm).

1. Place the knitted panel under a damp cloth and press, with the iron on a wool setting.

2. With right sides together, pin and machine stitch the knitted panel to the fabric rectangle, leaving a gap of about 6 in. (15 cm) along one side. Cut off the corners and turn right side out. Press.

3. Cut two circles of cardstock 3 in. (7.5 cm) in diameter, with a smaller circle ¾ in. (2 cm) in diameter cut out of the center of each one. Following the instructions on page 105, make four pompoms in different colors and trim them to neaten, leaving the yarn that is tied around the middle of the pom-pom long.

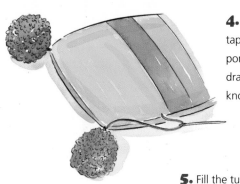

4. Thread the long ties through a tapestry needle and stitch one pom-pom at each corner of the draft excluder, finishing with a knot inside the tube.

5. Fill the tube with polyester toy filling or kapok to form a nice, round shape (see page 110) and whipstitch the gap closed (see page 111).

Pom-pom draft excluder

Pom-poms are great fun to make and also a good way to use up leftover yarn. For a children's room, why not glue felt eyes onto one end to make a fluffy caterpillar?

You will need

4 x 4-oz (100-g) balls of thick yarn in different colors

Cardstock

Tapestry needle

1. Using a compass and pencil, draw two circles 6¼ in. (16 cm) in diameter on cardstock. Draw a smaller circle 1½ in. (4 cm) in diameter in the center of each one. Cut out the smaller circles and then cut around the larger ones to give you two doughnut shapes. Cut out a section of about ¾ in. (2 cm).

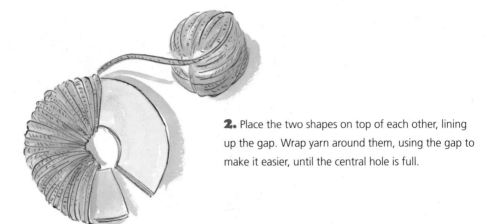

2. Place the two shapes on top of each other, lining up the gap. Wrap yarn around them, using the gap to make it easier, until the central hole is full.

3. Using scissors, cut around the outside, slipping the blade between the two cardstock discs.

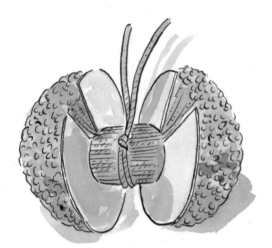

4. Cut a 24-in. (60-cm) length of yarn and tie it around the center of the pom-pom, pulling it between the cardboard disks. Tie a tight double knot. Carefully pull the cardstock disks off the pom-pom. Repeat steps 2 through 4 to make eight pom-poms in total. Trim all the pom-poms into neat, round shapes.

5. Thread a tapestry needle with a double length of yarn, tie a knot in the end, and stitch through the pom-poms to join them together. Make sure that you stitch right through the center of each one, so that they will sit securely in the finished draft excluder, and push the pom-poms up close to each other. Stitch through all the pom-poms again with a second length of doubled yarn for a more secure finish.

Patchwork draft excluder

This cute patchwork draft excluder is a great way to use up scraps of your favorite fabrics. To make the draft excluder really heavy, make a lining bag using two 35½ x 8¼-in. (88 x 21-cm) pieces of fabric: stitch them together leaving a small opening, turn right side out, fill with sand; stitch the opening closed and push the lining inside the patchwork tube.

You will need

Patterns on page 124

Cardstock for templates

Paper for patches (newspaper works well)

Scraps of fabric (enough for 32 hexagons)

8½ x 35 in. (21 x 88 cm) fabric for backing

Polyester toy filling or kapok

Take ⅜-in. (1-cm) seam allowances throughout, unless otherwise stated.

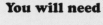

1. Enlarge the patterns on page 124 to twice the size and cut out. Cut a large and a small hexagon from cardstock to use as templates. Draw around the small template on paper 32 times and cut out. Using a rotary cutter and ruler, cut around the large hexagon to make 32 fabric hexagons.

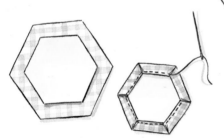

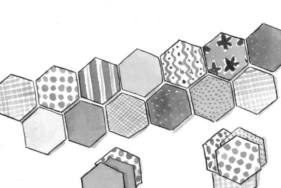

2. Lay a paper hexagon in the middle of a fabric one and fold the fabric over, pressing as you go with a cool iron, until all the sides are folded in. Baste (tack) around the hexagon, starting and finishing with a few small stitches. Do this with all the paper and fabric hexagons. Press them all again.

3. Lay the hexagons on your work surface and arrange them in three rows of 11, 10, and 11 hexagons respectively, moving them around until you are happy with the arrangement. Make sure that no two hexagons of the same fabric are next to each other.

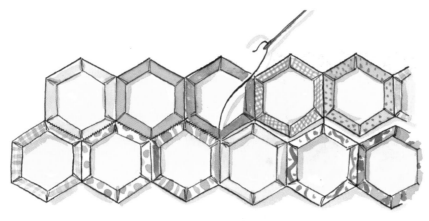

4. Starting along the bottom edge, stitch the hexagon patches together by oversewing the edges. Sew the bottom row together, then the middle row, and finally the top row. Stitch the rows together until you have a panel of patchwork.

5. Carefully remove the basting (tacking) stitches and take out the backing papers. Trim the panel to 8½ x 35 in. (21 x 88 cm) and press on the right side.

6. Cut a piece of backing fabric measuring 8¼ x 35½ in. (21 x 88 cm). With right sides together, pin and machine stitch the backing fabric to the patchwork panel, leaving a gap of about 5 in. (12 cm) at one end. Turn right side out and press.

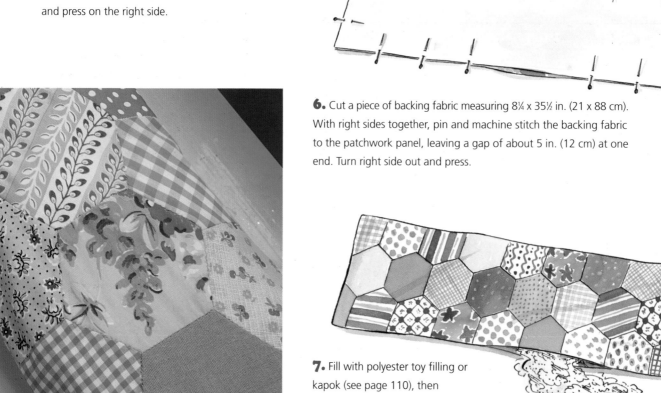

7. Fill with polyester toy filling or kapok (see page 110), then whipstitch the gap closed (see page 111).

Techniques

Cutting fabric

Before you start on a project, make sure that you have a good pair of sharp dressmaking scissors, which will make cutting the fabrics much easier and ensure that the cuts that you make are accurate.

When pinning the pattern pieces to the fabric, position the pattern as close to the edges of the fabric as you can, making sure that you avoid the selvage (selvedge). This will ensure that you use your fabric as economically as possible. If you need two of any one shape, fold the fabric over to double it and pin the pattern in place. I like to keep even quite small scraps of fabric that are left over, as they often come in handy for other projects.

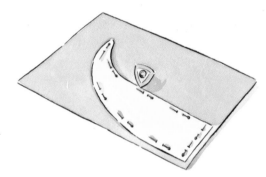

Cutting one shape at a time

To cut a shape using a paper pattern piece, pin the paper to the fabric, draw around it with tailor's chalk, then remove the pins and pattern, and cut out. This is the best method if the pattern is a complicated shape and you are only cutting through one layer of fabric. Alternatively, pin the pattern in place and cut around it, making sure that you do not cut into the paper.

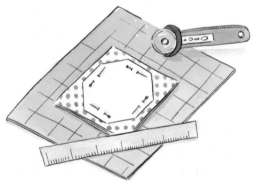

Cutting several of the same shape

To cut out several of the same shape, a rotary cutter and cutting mat (available from haberdashery stores) are very useful. Pin the pattern onto several layers of fabric (how many will depend on the thickness of the fabrics) and cut around it using the rotary cutter and a metal ruler.

Clipping notches in a curved seam

This technique takes just a couple of minutes to do and makes a real difference to the look of your sewing, as it helps curved seams lie flat.

On curved seams, simply clip into the seam allowance after stitching, taking care not to cut through any of the stitches. For inward curves, cut wedge-shaped notches; for outward curves, little slits will suffice.

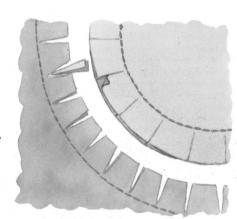

Making a strap or handle

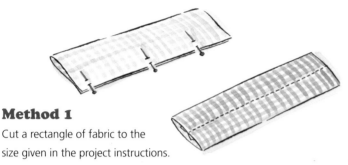

Method 1

Cut a rectangle of fabric to the size given in the project instructions. Fold it in half lengthwise, right sides together, and machine stitch along the long raw edge. Press the seam open. Turn the strip right side out and press, with the seam running down the center of one side.

Method 2

Cut two rectangles of fabric to the size given in the project instructions. With right sides together, pin and machine stitch the strips together along both long edges. Turn right side out and press. You can then topstitch along each long edge if you so wish.

Stuffing your doorstops

After much experimentation, I found that filling the doorstops about two thirds full with toy filling and then filling the remaining space with dried peas or lentils ensured that they kept their shape nicely and were heavy enough to prop an average-sized door open. If you require a more heavyweight doorstop, use less toy stuffing and more of the dried peas or lentils. Sand or uncooked rice could also be used, although the seams will need to be well stitched with no tiny gaps. And adding a handful of dried lavender is a nice touch, especially if you are making the doorstop as a gift.

Polyester toy filling is widely available and is very easy to use, giving a nice, smooth finish. Kapok can also be used if you can get hold of it; it gives a more solid, heavier finish.

For draft excluders for internal doors, use toy filling to form a compact, solid shape; for a heavier finish, add dried peas or similar as well. For an external door, fill the draft excluder with sand, as dried peas or lentils would absorb moisture.

To fill the doorstop, push small pieces of the stuffing that you are using into the fabric casing, making sure that it forms a nice shape. Then, using a jug or funnel (or a piece of paper rolled up and secured with tape), pour dried peas or similar into the remaining space.

When the doorstop is completely full, turn the edges of the opening inside by ⅜ in. (1 cm) and whipstitch (see page 111) the opening closed, using small, neat stitches and starting and finishing with a few small stitches to secure them in place.

Hand stitches

Running stitch

The simplest stitch there is, but it never loses its charm.

Bring the needle up at A, down at B, and up at C. Repeat, bringing the needle up and back down through the fabric several times along the stitching line. Try to space the stitches evenly and make them all the same length.

Backstitch

The ultimate utility stitch before the sewing machine was invented, this stitch can also be used decoratively to embroider flower stems.

Working from right to left, bring the needle up at A, down at B, and up at C, one stitch length ahead of A.

Whipstitch

This quick-to-work stitch is used to join fabrics right sides together and to close gaps in seams after you've stuffed your doorstops.

Hold the fabrics that are being joined right sides together. Bring the needle up on the front of the work, hiding the knot in between the two layers, than take the needle and thread to the back of the work and insert it from back to front. Pull through to complete the stitch. Take care not to loop the thread under the needle tip, otherwise you'll end up working a blanket stitch!

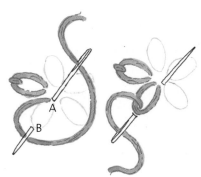

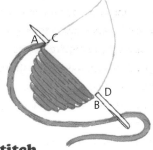

Lazy daisy stitch

This stitch gives you single loops, which make great flowers.

Bring the needle up at A, then loop the thread from left to right and insert the needle at A again. Bring it up at B, looping the thread under the needle tip. To finish off the stitch, take the needle down just outside the loop, forming a little bar or "tie."

French knot

This stitch forms a little knot, or bobble, on the surface of the fabric. It is useful for flower centers.

Bring the needle up, wrap the thread tightly around it twice, insert the needle as close to the point at which it first emerged as possible, and pull it through. (You may find it easiest to hold the wraps down with the thumbnail of your non-sewing hand.)

Satin stitch

Great for working features such as eyes, cheeks, and even hair.

Bring the needle up at A, down at B, up at C, down at D, and so on, working the stitches close together so that no fabric shows in between them.

Patterns

Seam allowances are included on all patterns where necessary;
refer to the individual project instructions for more information.

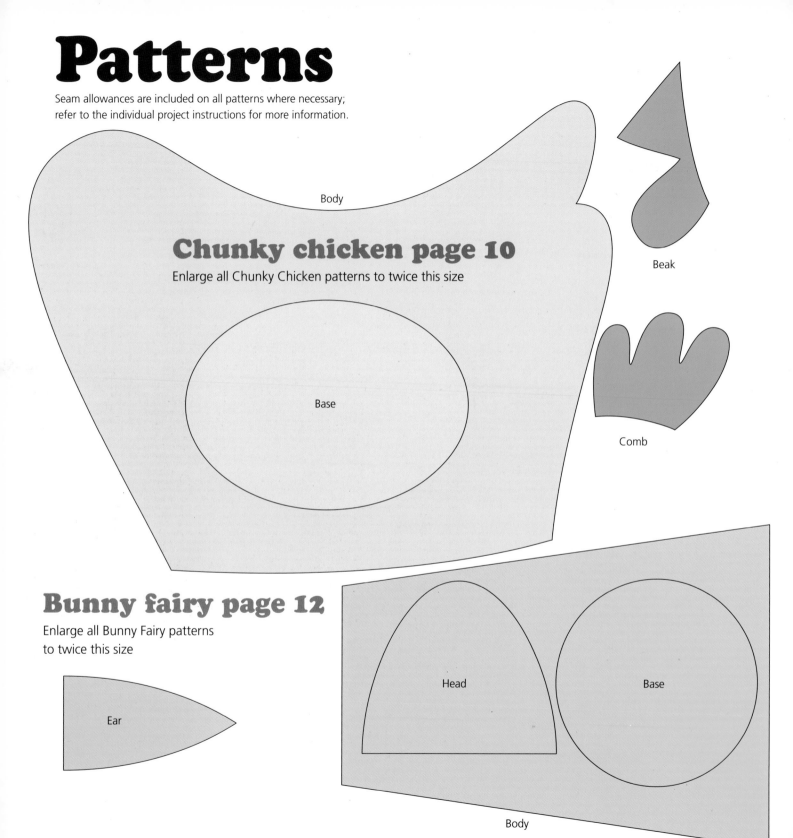

Body

Beak

Chunky chicken page 10

Enlarge all Chunky Chicken patterns to twice this size

Base

Comb

Bunny fairy page 12

Enlarge all Bunny Fairy patterns
to twice this size

Ear

Head

Base

Body

Cat page 16

Enlarge all Cat patterns to twice this size

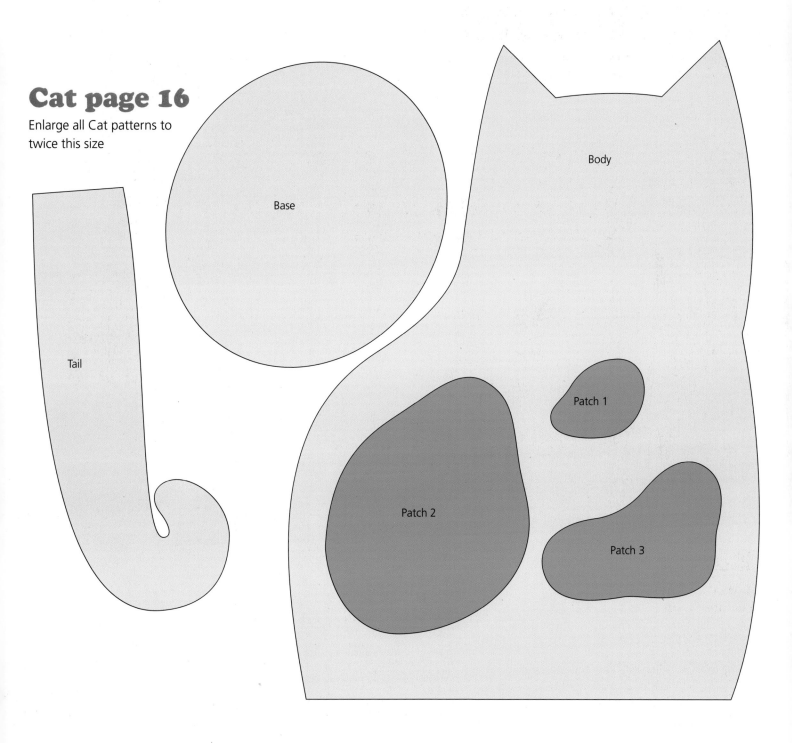

Base

Body

Tail

Patch 1

Patch 2

Patch 3

Dylan dog page 19

Enlarge all Dylan Dog patterns to twice this size

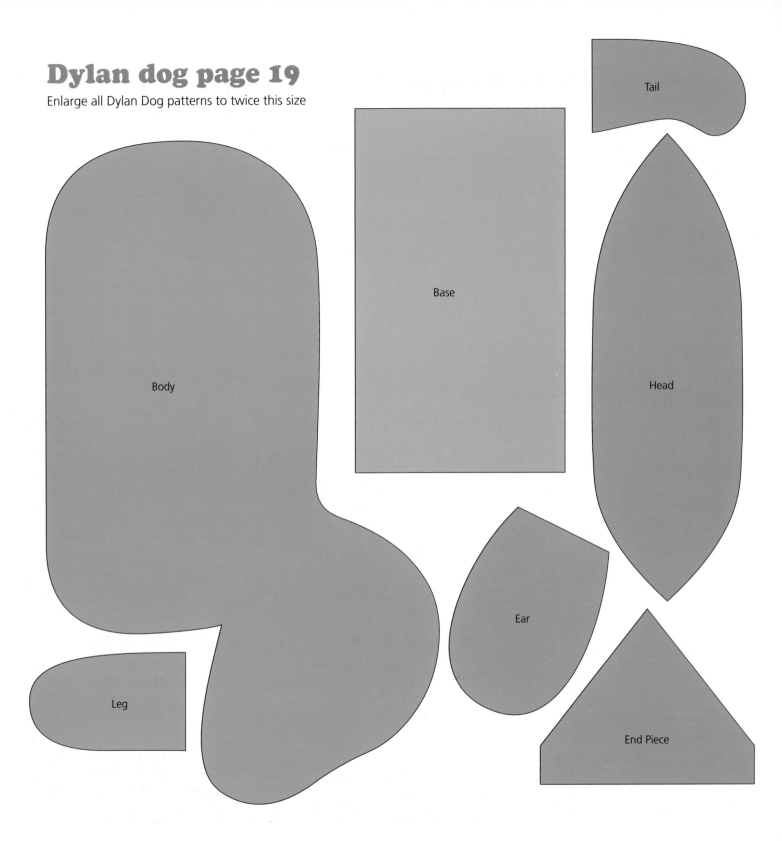

Tail

Base

Head

Body

Ear

Leg

End Piece

Appliquéd robot page 22

Enlarge all Appliquéd Robot patterns to twice this size

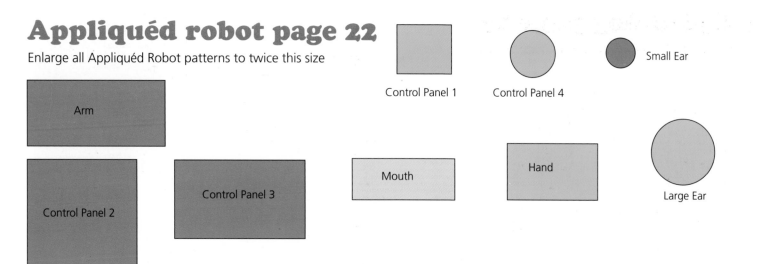

Control Panel 1

Control Panel 4

Small Ear

Arm

Control Panel 2

Control Panel 3

Mouth

Hand

Large Ear

Russian doll page 26

Enlarge all Russian Doll patterns to twice this size

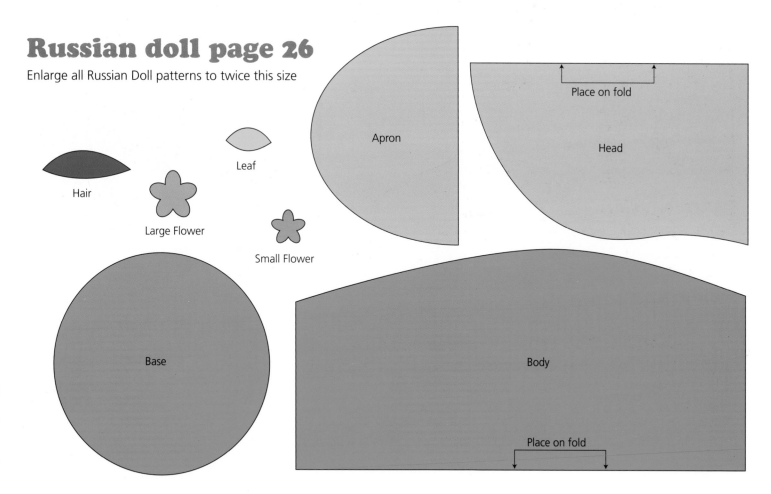

Hair

Leaf

Large Flower

Small Flower

Apron

Place on fold

Head

Base

Body

Place on fold

Dotty dachshund page 29

Enlarge all dachshund patterns to twice this size

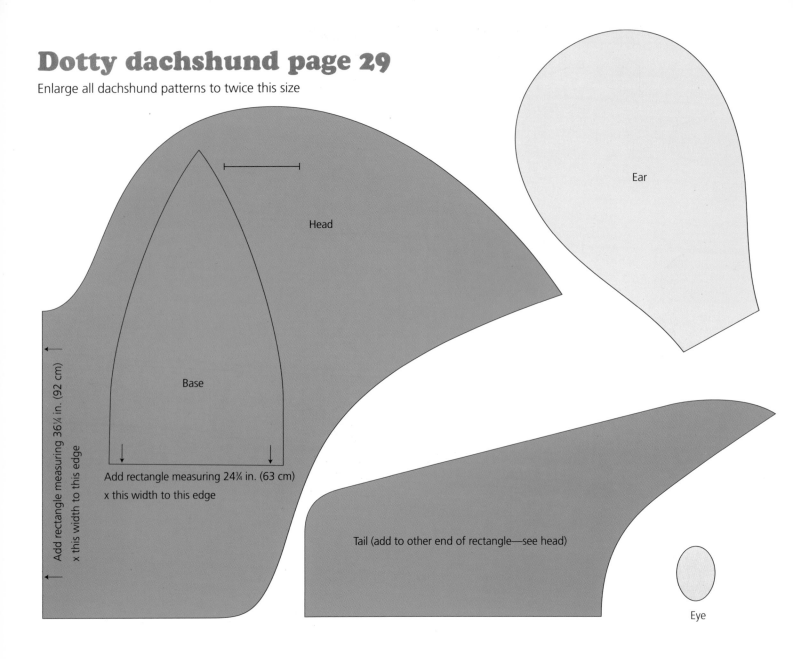

Ear

Head

Base

Add rectangle measuring 36¼ in. (92 cm) x this width to this edge

Add rectangle measuring 24¾ in. (63 cm) x this width to this edge

Tail (add to other end of rectangle—see head)

Eye

Sock monster page 32

Enlarge both Sock Monster patterns to twice this size

Eye

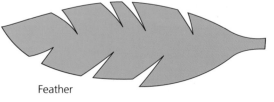

Feather

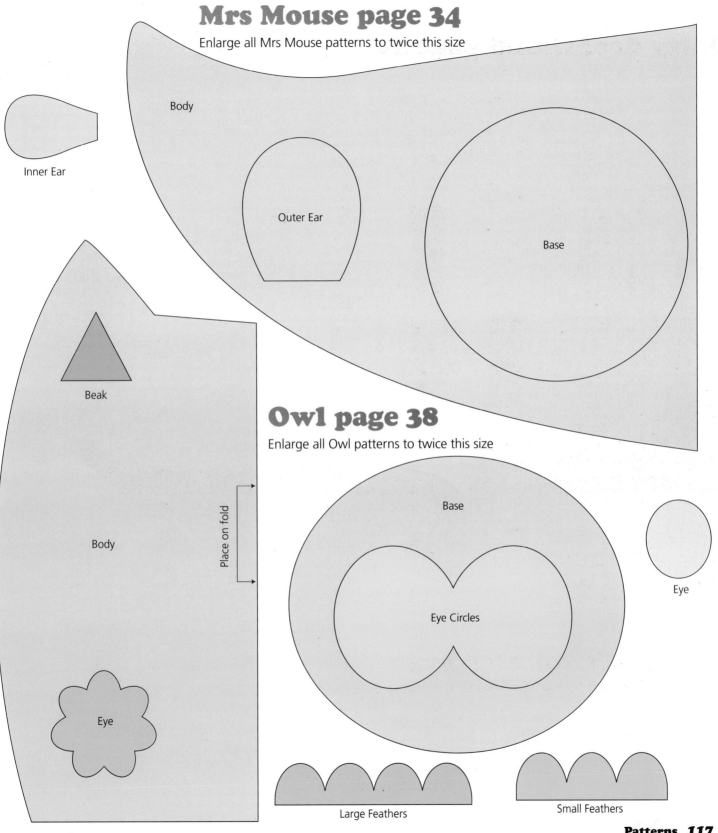

Mrs Mouse page 34

Enlarge all Mrs Mouse patterns to twice this size

Inner Ear

Body

Outer Ear

Base

Owl page 38

Enlarge all Owl patterns to twice this size

Beak

Body

Place on fold

Eye

Base

Eye Circles

Eye

Large Feathers

Small Feathers

Doll page 40

Enlarge all Doll patterns to twice this size

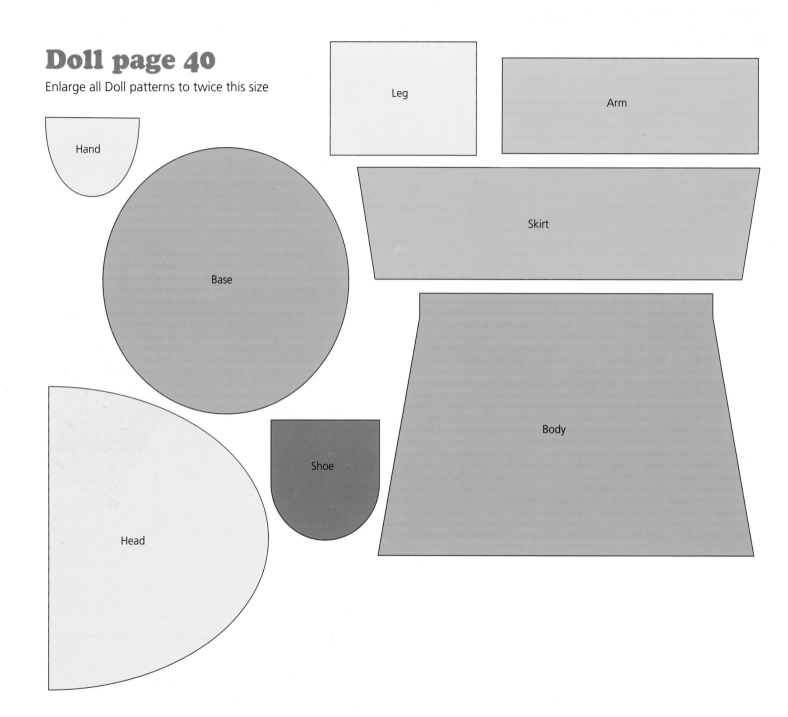

Leg

Arm

Hand

Skirt

Base

Body

Shoe

Head

Birdhouse page 44

Enlarge all Birdhouse patterns to twice this size

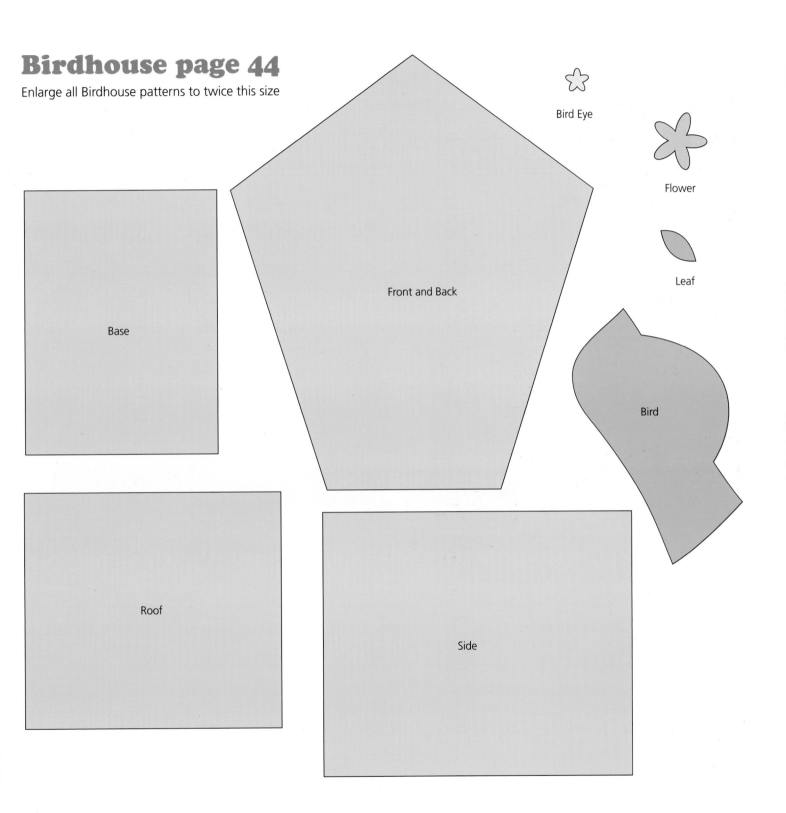

Bird Eye

Flower

Leaf

Base

Front and Back

Bird

Roof

Side

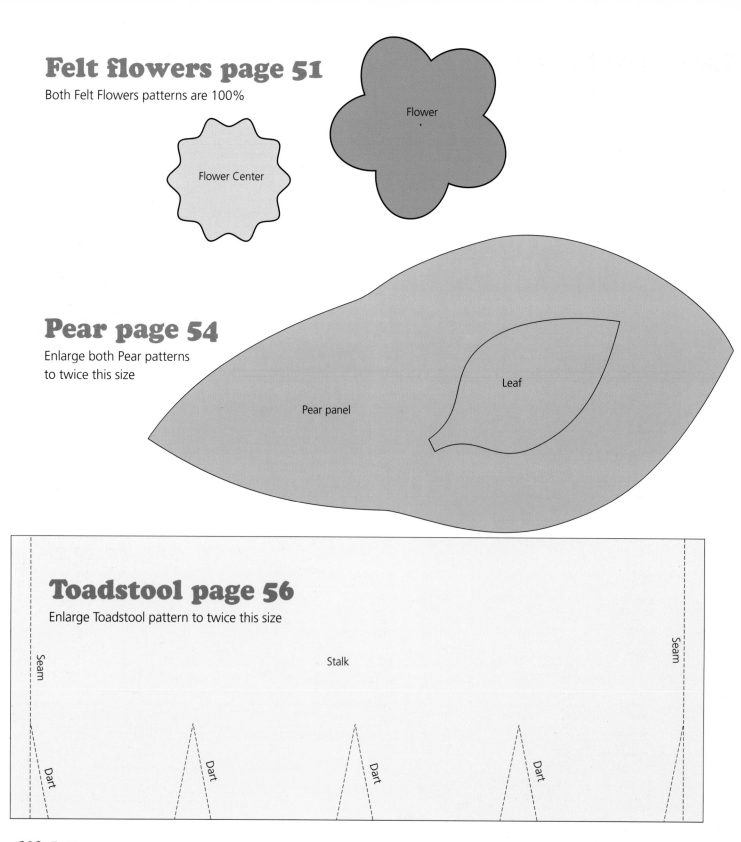

Felt flowers page 51

Both Felt Flowers patterns are 100%

Flower Center

Flower

Pear page 54

Enlarge both Pear patterns
to twice this size

Pear panel

Leaf

Toadstool page 56

Enlarge Toadstool pattern to twice this size

Seam

Stalk

Seam

Dart

Dart

Dart

Dart

Flowerpot page 59

Enlarge all Flowerpot patterns to twice this size

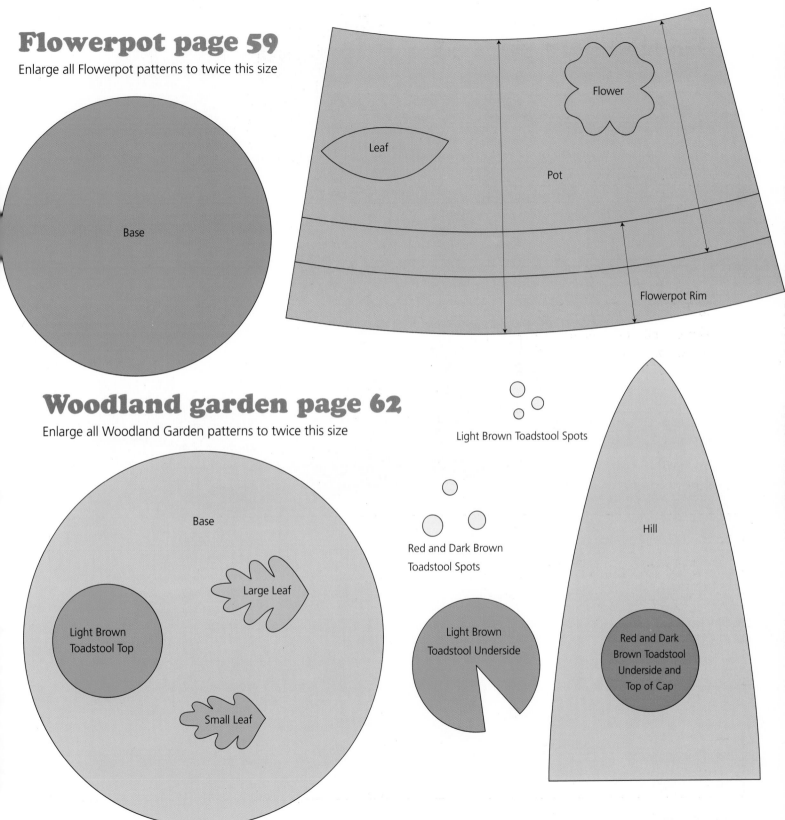

Base

Leaf

Flower

Pot

Flowerpot Rim

Woodland garden page 62

Enlarge all Woodland Garden patterns to twice this size

Light Brown Toadstool Spots

Red and Dark Brown
Toadstool Spots

Base

Large Leaf

Light Brown
Toadstool Top

Small Leaf

Light Brown
Toadstool Underside

Hill

Red and Dark
Brown Toadstool
Underside and
Top of Cap

Cute cupcake page 66

Enlarge all Cute Cupcake patterns to twice this size

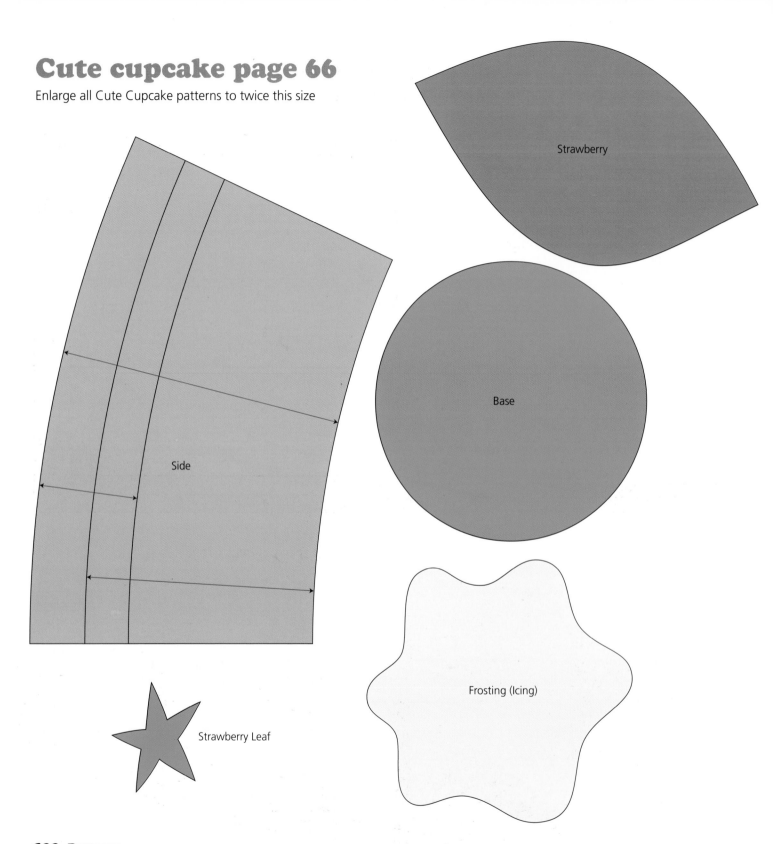

Strawberry

Base

Side

Frosting (Icing)

Strawberry Leaf

Pyramids page 72

Enlarge all Pyramids patterns to twice this size

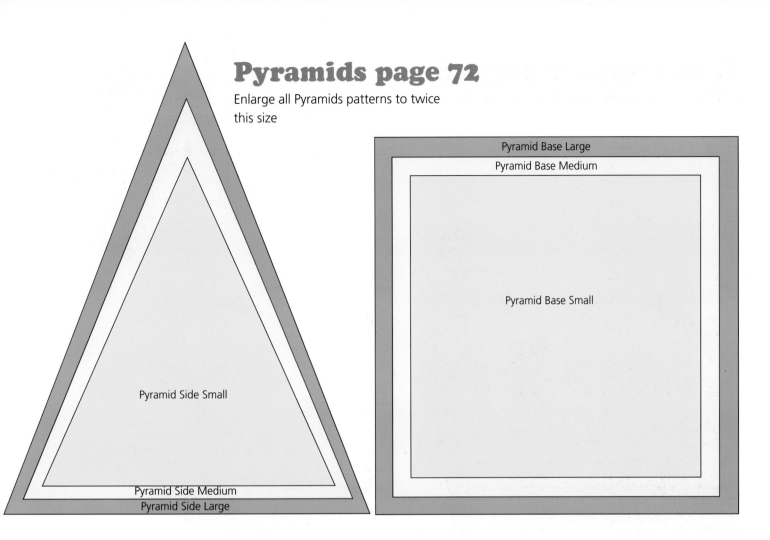

Pyramid Base Large
Pyramid Base Medium
Pyramid Base Small

Pyramid Side Small
Pyramid Side Medium
Pyramid Side Large

Rocket page 74

Enlarge all Rocket patterns to twice this size

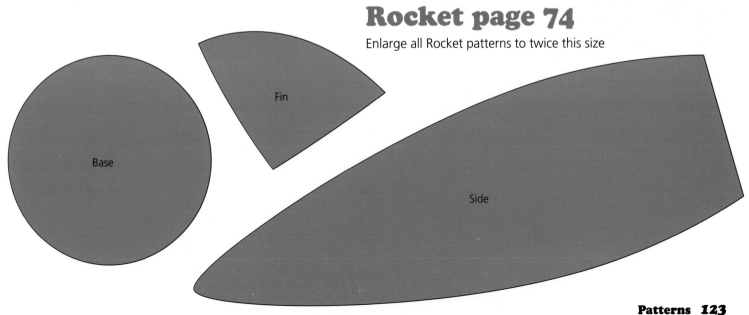

Base

Fin

Side

Purse page 82

Enlarge all Purse patterns to twice this size

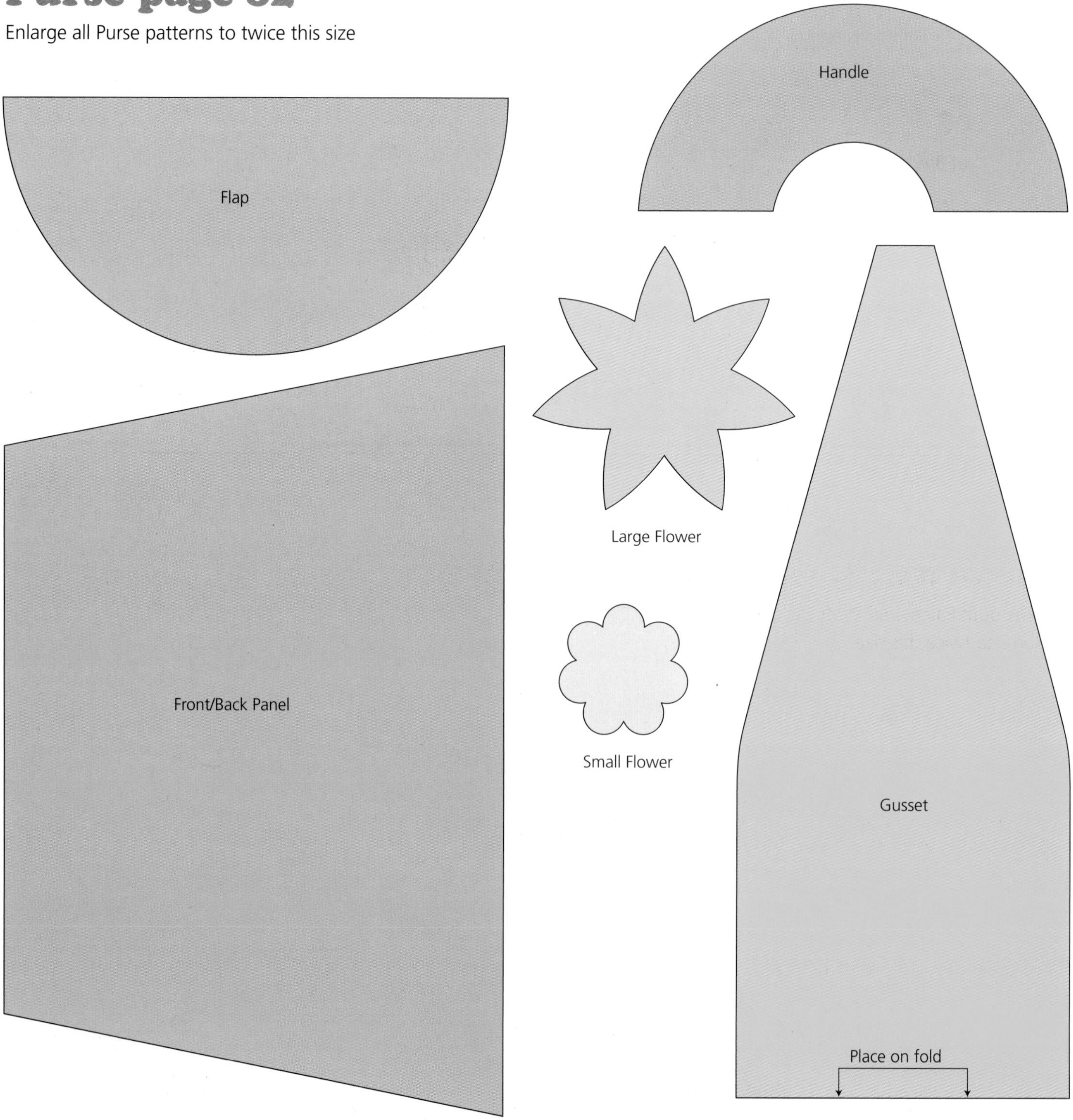

Flap

Handle

Large Flower

Small Flower

Front/Back Panel

Gusset

Place on fold

Velvet ball page 86

Enlarge Velvet Ball pattern to twice this size

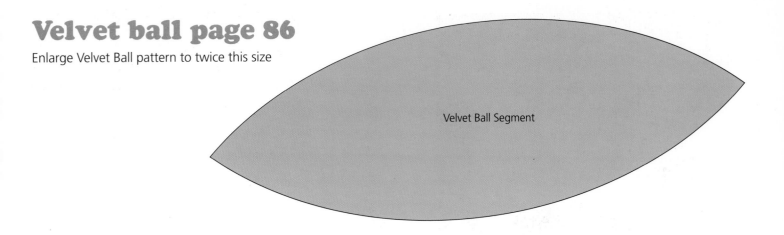

Velvet Ball Segment

Patchwork draft excluder page 106

Enlarge both Patchwork Draft Excluder
patterns to twice this size

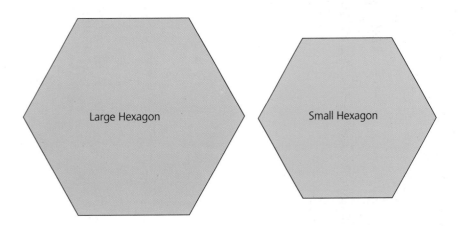

Large Hexagon

Small Hexagon

Gingerbread house page 92

Enlarge all Gingerbread House patterns to twice this size

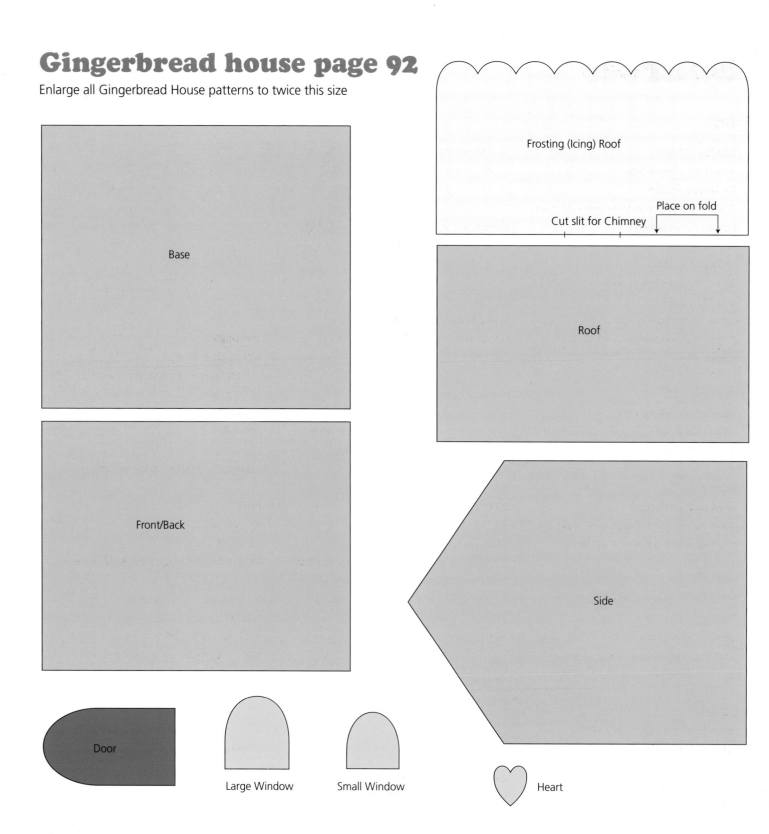

Frosting (Icing) Roof

Cut slit for Chimney

Place on fold

Base

Roof

Front/Back

Side

Door

Large Window

Small Window

Heart

Sources

UK

DONNA FLOWER
www.donnaflower.com
Tel: 07896 922694
Great online selection of vintage fabrics and notions (haberdashery).

FABRICS GALORE
52–54 Lavender Hill, London SW11 5RH
020 7738 9589
www.fabricsgalore.co.uk
A brilliant, ever-changing selection of fabrics.

FABRIC REHAB
www.fabricrehab.co.uk
Lovely online collection of contemporary patterned fabrics.

HOBBYCRAFT
www.hobbycraft.co.uk
Great for notions (haberdashery) and craft supplies, with branches nationwide.

JOHN LEWIS
300 Oxford Street, London W1A 1EX
Tel: 020 7629 7711
www.johnlewis.com
Wide selection of notions (haberdashery) and craft materials.

LIBERTY
Regent Street, London W1B 5AH
Tel: 020 7734 1234
www.liberty.co.uk
Beautiful own print fabrics and beautiful range of ribbons and braids.

THE MAKE LOUNGE
49–51 Barnsbury Street, London N1 1TP
Tel: 020 7609 0275
www.themakelounge.com
Fabrics, notions (haberdashery), craft books and magazines, also sewing and craft courses.

PAPER-AND-STRING
www.paper-and-string.co.uk
A brilliant selection of colored felts and a wide range of buttons and ribbons.

SAINTS & PINNERS
www.saintsandpinners.co.uk
A wide range of contemporary patterned fabrics.

RAY STITCH
99 Essex Road, London N1 2SJ
Tel: 020 7704 1060
www.raystitch.co.uk
Large selection of contemporary fabrics with beautiful notions (haberdashery).

US

BRITEX FABRICS
146 Geary Street, San Francisco CA 94108
Tel: (415) 392 2910
www.britexfabrics.com
Wide range of fabrics and notions.

AMY BUTLER
www.amybutlerdesign.com
Fantastic collections of fabrics.

CIA'S PALETTE
www.ciaspalette.com
A large selection of modern and quilting fabrics.

FABDIR
www.fabdir.com
Claims to be the world's largest online fabric store directory.

HOBBY LOBBY
www.hobbylobby.com
Craft and hobby supplies; stores nationwide.

JOANN FABRIC & CRAFT STORES
Tel: 888-739-4120
www.joann.com
Craft and hobby supplies; stores nationwide.

MICHAELS
Tel: 800-642-4235
www.michaels.com
Craft and hobby supplies; stores nationwide.

A.C. MOORE
Tel: 888-226-6673
www.acmoore.com
Craft and hobby supplies; stores nationwide.

PURL SOHO
459 Broome Street, New York NY10013
Tel: (212) 420 8796
www.purlsoho.com
Great range of fabrics, notions, and craft tools.

Index

Acknowledgments

Thank you so much to Debbie Patterson for taking such great photographs, Michael Hill for all the beautiful illustrations, Sarah Hoggett for calm and efficient editing, Louise Leffler for the great design, Sally Powell for organizing locations and much more, Pete Jorgensen for pulling it all together, and Cindy Richards for commissioning the book in the first place. And thank you to Laurie, Gracie and Betty for continuing love and support.